D0542327

JAPANESE

FOR

BEGINNERS

●日本語入門

Authors:

Yasuo YOSHIDA (Overall supervision)
    Professor Emeritus, OSAKA UNIVERSITY OF FOREIGN STUDIES
Shunsuke OKUNISHI (Last three pages of each UNIT)
    OSAKA UNIVERSITY OF FOREIGN STUDIES
Nao'omi KURATANI (First three pages of each UNIT)
    SHOIN WOMEN'S UNIVERSITY

Editorial Adviser:

Tetsuo SHIBATA
    Professor Emeritus, OSAKA UNIVERSITY

GAKKEN

JAPANESE FOR BEGINNERS
©GAKKEN 1976
Published by Gakken Co., Ltd.
4-40-5, Kami-ikedai, Ohta-ku, Tokyo 145, Japan
ISBN4-05-151310-6
Printed in Japan
All rights reserved.
No part of this book may be reproduced in any form
without the written permission of the publisher.

First published 1976
Thirty-second impression 1989

PRODUCTION STAFF
English Consultants
Frederick M. Uleman
James R. Abrams
Layout & Design
Junichiro Magoshi
Illustration
Hidetsugu Muraki
Gakken Co., Ltd.
Yoshio Tanaka
Masayoshi Okubo

PREFACE

With the acceleration of interchange between Japan and other nations, the needs of communication expand from the diplomatic, business and academic world of the technocratic elite to the everyday exchange of thoughts and ideas among the working populaces. Among the linguistically updated and pedagogically workable textbooks continually sought in the field of Japanese as a Second Language (JASL), we are experiencing demand for more intense concentration in the area of aural-oral skills. *Japanese for Beginners* is Gakken's response to this particular need with a simplified text providing for basic conversational competence in practical, efficient lessons. While Gakken's *Japanese for Today* has been widely accepted and adopted for classroom/self study use as a three-skill oriented text (aural, oral and reading comprehension) both internal and external to Japan, *Japanese for Beginners* is aimed primarily at strengthening aural and oral skills—two basic linguistic tools for conversation.

The overall organization of the text—the layout and planning of the entire 30 lessons—is such that each lesson follows an identical pagination and activity schedule. This feature assures familiarity with lesson activity progression and expedites review and reference. Designed for function and utility, lesson content does not attempt to be exhaustive or technical. Explanations and grammatical rules given in succinct English are easily understandable and sufficient for self study. For the innovative instructor with the luxury of time, each lesson provides a framework for more extensive development of basic patterns, grammar and vocabulary. Another innovative feature is its possible use as a dictionary substitute. There being few Romanized dictionaries available, use of the "New Words" section and the "Index" in close reference with each other serves to facilitate learning not only in the use of this volume but also in the higher levels of textbooks succeeding.

Japanese for Beginners, with its solid pedagogical content, also strives to raise the learner's motivation and interest by incorporating cultural aspects and innovative organizational features. Attractively accentuated by graphic and photographic illustrations, it is prepared with the hope that the learner may continue on to higher levels of competence about the culture behind the language as well as in performance in the language itself.

Yukiko S. Jolly, Ph.D.
University of Hawaii

ACKNOWLEDGMENTS

As is well known, there is no royal road to learning a language, only the plebeian path of practice, practice, and more practice. However, with a good guide, this can also be the road to new adventures.

Because language tends to be thought of overseas as vocalization of feelings, this text has foregone the traditional Japanese emphasis on Chinese characters and instead put the primary emphasis on the easier-to-learn and more-immediately-useful conversational language. By the same token, of course, this neglect of the written forms makes good pronunciation and intonation in conversation all the more important. Tape and real-life practice are essential.

Nevertheless, repetition is not the purpose. The goal is fluency and the means is well-rounded practice concentrating on the most useful words, phrases, and sentence patterns of everyday life, beginning with the elementary and working up to the more advanced. Difficult points being explained in academically sound detail to advance your understanding and to enhance your ability, every effort has been made to make your study as easy as the requirements of the language allow. For example, related grammatical patterns are grouped and explained around common themes. Charts summarizing and comparing the different adverbials, verbs, and postpositions also facilitate "natural" learning. You are especially urged to read the section on How To Use This Book to take best advantage of these many special features.

Finally, the authors would like to acknowledge the invaluable assistance of some of the people who helped this project come to fruition. Special mention must go to Professor Tetsuo Shibata for his pioneering work and guidance and to Professor Yukiko S. Jolly of the University of Hawaii for her gracious preface. We are also indebted to Frederick M. Uleman and James R. Abrams for their counsel and efforts in rewriting our English to say what we wanted it to. Lastly, but nonetheless indispensable, are the many people at Gakken who have encouraged us on in this task. To them, and to other friends and associates too numerous to list, we are sincerely grateful.

Yasuo Yoshida

CONTENTS

How To Use This Book

All together, there are thirty Study Units in this book, each Unit six pages long.

The first page of the Unit starts with the Key Structures. Look at these Key Sentences and try to understand them, if necessary referring to the translations on the next page or to the vocabulary on the previous page. The Key Sentences are followed by the Basic Constructions and grammatical explanations. In understanding these stylized representations of the grammar, it will often be helpful to refer to the Further Study on the third page of the Unit.

Going on to the second page of the Unit, you have More Examples For Practice. By now, you should be able to understand these in Japanese, and the translations that are given are simply so that you can check your own understanding.

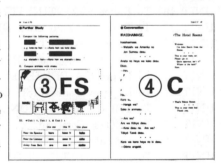

On page three is the Further Study which gives detailed explanations or reviews important and difficult points in the Unit. You have already looked at this in connection with the Key Structures, so just read it again to make sure you understand it.

Page four has the Conversation using all of these Basic Constructions and vocabulary words. These Conversations follow an American traveler from his arrival at New Tokyo International Airport to his final departure in Unit 30. The Conversations are easy and natural, and accompanied by English translations.

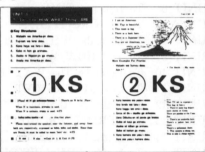

Turning next to page five of the Unit, you will find the Look & Learn. This is a graphic presentation of vocabulary and other points, and can be used both for building your vocabulary and for practicing the Basic Constructions.

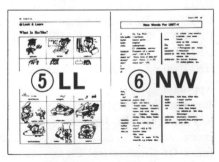

Page six of the Unit has a list of New Words for the next Unit. Look at this and try to memorize these words. If you are able to learn the new words which will be used in the next Unit ahead of time, it will be that much easier to understand the next Unit.

In Addition, there are also a number of special features to help you use this text to best advantage, among them the vocabulary Index (→Appendix), the Reverse Index of Verb Conjugations (→p. 128), and the Summary of Homonymous Postpositionals (→p. 158).

Finally, special mention must be made of the set of two cassette tapes. These tapes include all Key Sentences, pattern practices, and Conversations, plus a section for pronunciation practice. They are an invaluable aid to your mastery of the spoken language.

Abbreviations and Notations

A	Stem of A·i Adjective	V^C	Consonant-ending Verb →U-8 ②
Adj	Adjective or Adjectival	Vi	intransitive verb
Adv	Adverb or Adverbial	V^M	V·masu, V·masen, etc. →U-9 FS
A·i	Adjective ending in ·i		
C	Consonant	V^P	V·u, V·nai, etc. →U-14 FS
Cf.	Compare	Vt	transitive verb
Cph	Conversational phrase	V^V	Vowel-ending Verb →U-8 ②
FS	Further Study	Vw	Vowel
KS	Key Structure	V^X	Irregular Verb →U-8 ②
LL	Look & Learn	NB:	*nota bene* ⟨Note well⟩
N	Noun	➡, →	See
Na	Adjective taking -na as its connector	←	derived from or originated in
N(a)	Stem of Na Adjective	／	or
Nv	Noun which can be used as a Verb with the addition of -suru; e.g. sanpo ⟨a walk⟩ →sanpo-suru ⟨to take a walk⟩	·	ending indicating a V or A
		( )	can be omitted
		[ ]	category
		⟨ ⟩	translation; reference
		...	omission of words
pl.	plural	·	omission of morphemes
sing.	singular	～	omission of sounds
U	Unit; e.g. U-1: Unit 1		
V	Verb in stem form		

How To Pronounce Japanese

In this book, the Roman alphabet is used to describe the Japanese language in order to make it easier for English speakers to learn, although Japanese is almost always written in Chinese ideograms and syllabic characters, these to be briefly introduced in Unit 28, Unit 29, and the Appendix.

A rough guide to pronunciation is given below with an explanation of the orthographic system used in this book. It is primarily intended, however, not as an exhaustive account of Japanese phonetics but as an aid to help the would-be speaker attain an intelligible pronunciation without the assistance of a native teacher.

1. Sounds of Letters

	Letters	Approximate pronunciation
Consonants	b	as in *b*uck
	ch	as in *ch*uck →NB 1)
	d	as in *d*uck
	f	between *f*ood and *h*ood →NB 2)
	g	as in *g*ood or si*ng*er →NB 3)
	h	as in *h*am
	j	as in *j*am
	k	as in *k*ite
	m	as in *m*ight
	n	as in *n*ight and e*n*plane or e*m*plane before p, b, or m
	p	as in S*p*ain
	r	similar to *r*ain, *l*ain, or *d*eign →NB 4)
	s	as in *s*ame
	sh	as in *sh*ame →NB 1)
	t	as in *t*ights
	ts	as in tigh*ts* →NB 1)
	w	as in *w*ag →NB 5)
	z	as in *z*one
Semivowel	y	as in *y*ap
Vowels	a	as in p*a*lm but short
	e	as in m*e*t
	i	as in t*ea* but short
	o	as in s*aw* but short
	u	as in n*oo*n but short →NB 6)

NB: 1) The clusters ch, sh, and ts are to be regarded as single consonants.
2) The sound f is a bilabial fricative.
3) The sound g is often pronounced as a velar nasal, unless it is the initial letter of the word. The Postpositional ga may often be pronounced as

a velar nasal, as though it were nga.

4) The sound r is pronounced with the tip of the tongue first touching briefly against the upper teeth ridge and then pulling downwards.

5) The sound w is to be regarded not as a semivowel but as a consonant.

6) The vowel u is pronounced with the lips unrounded, and is occasionally weakened, or omitted, typically when it comes at the end of the word.

7) The vowel clusters or diphthongs ei and ii are usually pronounced just like the extended monophthongs ē and ī respectively.

2. Signs

Signs	Orthographic functions
–	double duration; e.g. ā is to be pronounced for twice as long as a.
'	in n'a, n'e, etc., n and the following vowel or semivowel are to be pronounced separately, this to distinguish from the single-syllable na, ne, etc.
'	consequent dropping of the vowel o between n and d

3. Syllables and Beats

Unlike English, Japanese never has a consonant cluster in one syllable. Therefore, for example, the word matchi is to be broken into two syllables mat and chi ⟨→ p. 6 NB 1⟩, not ma and tchi. Japanese syllables can thus be categorized into the following four types: Vw, CVw, VwC, CVwC. ⟨Vw=vowel and C=consonant, this initial C including the semivowel y and the cluster 'C+y'.⟩

Beat plays an important role in natural pronunciation of Japanese. The system for counting beats has the following two rules:

(1) The beat unit consists of the syllables with short vowels ⟨Vw and CVw⟩.

(2) When the syllable has an extended vowel V̄w or ends with a consonant, it is counted as two beats.

Therefore, Japanese has eight types of syllabic beats as follows.

Syllables	Beats	Examples	Syllables	Beats	Examples
Vw	1	a–ka, e–ki	V̄w	2	ō–ki–i, ō–sa–ka
CVw	1	ka–ta, ki–ta	CV̄w	2	tō–kyō, sē–tā
VwC	2	at–ta, an–da	V̄wC	3	ōn–toki, ān–do–ran
CVwC	2	kat–ta, kit–ta	CV̄wC	3	tōt–ta, hōt–te

4. Accent

Unlike English, accent in Japanese is pitch accent rather than stress accent. Thus, instead of pronouncing a syllable louder, one or more beats of a word are pronounced at a higher pitch than the rest.

8

Let's Pronounce

TAPE ①-Ⓐ

Pronounce the following words aloud, paying careful attention to the beats and the pitches as indicated by the musical notes.

1.

a i
⟨love⟩

bi ru
⟨building⟩

chi zu
⟨map⟩

fu ne
⟨ship⟩

go go
⟨afternoon⟩

ha ha
⟨mother⟩

ne ko
⟨cat⟩

so ra
⟨sky⟩

u mi
⟨sea⟩

yo ru
⟨night⟩

2.

ga ka
⟨painter⟩

he ya
⟨room⟩

hi ru
⟨daytime⟩

ho shi
⟨star⟩

i e
⟨house⟩

ku ni
⟨country⟩

te ra
⟨temple⟩

tsu me
⟨nail⟩

ya ma
⟨mountain⟩

yu ki
⟨snow⟩

3.

da i ku
⟨carpenter⟩

ka na ri
⟨rather⟩

me ga mi
⟨goddess⟩

ni motsu
⟨baggage⟩

mu su me
⟨daughter⟩

no zo mi
⟨hope⟩

tsu ku e
⟨desk⟩

wa ta shi
⟨I⟩

a na ta
⟨you⟩

a o i
⟨blue⟩

hi to ri
⟨one person⟩

shi ka shi
⟨but⟩

4.

a i sa tsu
〈greeting〉

ma i ni chi
〈every day〉

ne ku ta i
〈necktie〉

ga i ko ku
〈foreign country〉

i ri gu chi
〈entrance〉

to mo da chi
〈friend〉

mi zu u mi
〈lake〉

o to to i
〈the day before yesterday〉

su zu shi i
〈cool〉

ko ko no tsu
〈nine〉

ku da mo no
〈fruit〉

ku tsu shi ta
〈socks〉

5.

pen
〈pen〉

den ki
〈electricity〉

hon da na
〈bookshelf〉

pin pon
〈ping-pong〉

san
〈three〉

rin go
〈apple〉

kan ga e

zen zen
〈not at all〉

6.

ryō ri
〈cooking〉

ryo kō
〈travel〉

sen se i
〈teacher〉

yū be
〈last night〉

byō ki
〈illness〉

kyū jū
〈ninety〉

nyū in
〈hospitalization〉

gyō ji
〈event〉

7.

gak kō
〈school〉

ik ka i
〈first floor〉

an na
〈like that〉

san nin
〈three persons〉

Nip pon
〈Japan〉

is shū kan
〈one week〉

it ta
〈went〉

kit te
〈postage stamp〉

8.

o ji i san
〈grandfather〉

o ji san
〈uncle〉

o bā san
〈grandmother〉

o ba san
〈aunt〉

mā ku
〈mark〉

ma ku
〈scatter〉

u ru
〈acquire〉

ū ru
〈wool〉

nē mu
〈name〉

ne mu
〈silk tree〉

tō ru
〈pass〉

to ru
〈take〉

9.

se ki
〈cough〉

sek ki
〈stone implement〉

i so
〈strand〉

is sō
〈still more〉

shi ta
〈did〉

shit ta
〈knew〉

su pa i
〈spy〉

sup pa i
〈sour〉

10.

kyō
〈today〉

ki yō
〈skillfulness〉

ki yō
〈appointment〉

ki ō
〈bygones〉

ryaku
〈abbreviation〉

ri ya ku
〈divine favor〉

kya ku
〈visitor〉

ki ya ku
〈agreement〉

hyō
〈leopard〉

hi yō
〈expense〉

byō in
〈hospital〉

bi yō in
〈beauty parlor〉

11.

ka ni
〈crab〉

kan' i
〈simplicity〉

a ni
〈older brother〉

an' i
〈easiness〉

an ni
〈tacitly〉

ki nen
〈commemoration〉

ki nen
〈prayer〉

kin' en
〈No Smoking〉

kin nen
〈recent years〉

New Words For UNIT 1

Amerika ←America, USA
anata you ⟨sing.⟩
anata-gata you ⟨pl.⟩
Arabia ←Arabia
are that →KS & U-15 FS
are-ra those →KS
Arigatō. ⟨Cph⟩ Thank you.
Arigatō gozaimasu. ⟨Cph⟩ Thank you.
 ⟨Polite⟩
asu tomorrow
biru ←building
Biru ←Bill
Burajiru ←Brazil
Chūgoku China
Dō-itashimashite. ⟨Cph⟩ You are wel-
 come.
Doitsu ⟨←Dutch *Duits*⟩ Germany
dōmo ⟨Cph⟩⟨Adv⟩ Thanks; very
 much ⟨before **arigatō**⟩
 Dōmo arigatō. Thank you
 very much.
Ei-go English language
Ejiputo ←Egypt
Emirī ←Emily
enpitsu pencil
Furansu ←France
-go ⟨Suffix for languages⟩
Gurīn ←Greene
Hai, Yes, →U-7 KS & FS
Igirisu ⟨←Portuguese *Inglez*⟩
 England
Iie, No, →U-7 KS & FS
inu dog
isu chair, sofa
-jin ⟨Suffix for peoples⟩
Jōnzu ←Jones
ka or →KS
Kanada ←Canada
Kaoru ⟨male or female name⟩

Konbanwa. ⟨Cph⟩ Good evening.
Konnichiwa. ⟨Cph⟩ Hello.; Good
 afternoon.
kore this →KS & U-15 FS
kore-ra these →KS
kyō today
neko cat
Nippon Japan (=Nihon)
Nyū-jīrando ←New Zealand
Ohayō. ⟨Cph⟩ Good morning.
Ohayō gozaimasu. ⟨Cph⟩ Good morning. ⟨Polite⟩
Ōsutoraria ←Australia
Oyasumi. ⟨Cph⟩ Good night.
Oyasumi-nasai. ⟨Cph⟩ Good night.
 ⟨Polite⟩
pen ←pen
Porutogaru ←Portugal
Roshia ⟨←Russian *Rossija*⟩
 Russia
-san Mr., Ms., Dear
Sayōnara. ⟨Cph⟩ Good-by.
sore that
So-ren USSR
sore-ra those →KS
Sumisu ←Smith
Supein ←Spain
-tachi ⟨Suffix to make plurals⟩
Tanaka ⟨family name: The family
 name comes first in Japa-
 nese.⟩
to and →KS
tsukue desk, table
watashi I
watashi-tachi we
ya and →KS

UNIT 1
To NAME Things

● Key Structures

1. watashi; watashi-tachi: anata; anata-gata
2. Amerika-jin to Nippon-jin
3. Igirisu-jin-tachi ya Kanada-jin-tachi
4. Ōsutoraria-jin ka Nyū-jīrando-jin
5. kore; sore; are: kore-ra; sore-ra; are-ra
6. Sumisu-san to Jōnzu-san

---

1 | [Person]→[Person]-**tachi** | [Person]→[Person], [Person], . . .

Japanese Nouns ⟨N⟩, generally, have no plural forms, neither do they take 'articles.' To stress plurality, put -tachi after Nouns indicating persons. An exception is: anata→anata-gata.

2 | N₁ **to** N₂ | N₁ and N₂ ➡FS

3 | N₁ **ya** N₂ | N₁, N₂, and others ➡FS

4 | N₁ **ka** N₂ | N₁ or N₂

5 | **kore; sore; are**

Japanese equivalents to the English 'this' and 'that' are kore, sore, and are. Kore indicates a thing near the speaker, sore near the listener, and are away from both ⟨➡FS⟩. -ra makes them plural.

6 | [Person]→[Person]-**san** | Mr./ Ms. / Dear [Person]

1. I; we: you ⟨sing.⟩; you ⟨pl.⟩

2. an American and a Japanese

3. Englishmen, Canadians, and others

4. an Australian or a New Zealander

5. this; that; that: these; those; those

6. Mr. Smith and Ms. Jones

★More Examples For Practice

1. watashi; watashi-**tachi**
   anata; anata-**gata**
   Amerika-jin; Amerika-jin-**tachi**

2. anata **to** watashi
   Igirisu-jin **to** Furansu-jin
   inu **to** neko

3. inu **ya** neko
   Nippon-jin **ya** Chūgoku-jin
   watashi-tachi **ya** anata-gata

4. Igirisu-jin **ka** Kanada-jin
   pen **ka** enpitsu
   kyō **ka** asu

5. **kore** to **sore** to **are**
   are ya **kore**
   are ka **sore**

6. Tanaka Kaoru-**san**
   Biru-**san** to Emirī-**san**
   Sumisu-**san** to Gurīn-**san**

---

1. I; we
   you ⟨sing.⟩; you ⟨pl.⟩
   an American; Americans
2. you and I
   an Englishman and a Frenchman
   a dog and a cat
3. dogs, cats, and other animals
   Japanese, Chinese, and others
   we, you, and the rest
4. an Englishman or a Canadian
   a pen or a pencil
   today or tomorrow
5. this, that, and that one there
   that, this, and others
   that one over there or that one
6. Mr./Mrs./Miss Kaoru Tanaka
   Bill and Emily
   Mr. Smith and Ms. Greene

● Further Study

I. Compare the usages of to and ya.

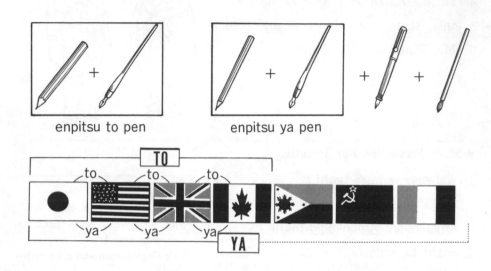

enpitsu to pen   enpitsu ya pen

II. Indicating things.

biru→ are

tsukue→ kore

isu→ sore

●Conversation

KONNICHIWA.—————————————————《Greetings》

Konnichiwa.

Konnichiwa, Sumisu-san.

* * *

Ohayō.

Ohayō gozaimasu.

* * *

Konbanwa.

* * *

Sayōnara.

* * *

Oyasumi.

Oyasumi-nasai.

* * *

Dōmo.

Arigatō.

Dōmo arigatō.

Dōmo arigatō gozaimasu.

* * *

Dō-itashimashite.

* * *

Hai.

Iie.

Hello.
Hello, Mr. Smith.
  * * *
Morning. 〈Familiar〉
Good morning. 〈Polite〉
  * * *
Good evening.
  * * *
Good-by.
  * * *
Good night. 〈Familiar〉
Good night. 〈Polite〉
  * * *
Thanks.
Thank you.
Thank you very much.
〈Familiar〉
Thank you very much.
〈Polite〉
  * * *
You are welcome.
  * * *
Yes.
No.

OHAYŌ!
OHAYŌ!

●Look & Learn

Nations, Peoples, Languages

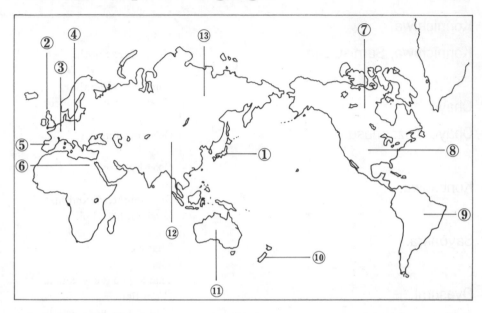

	Nation	People	Language
①	Nippon	Nippon-jin	Nippon-go
②	Igirisu	Igirisu-jin	Ei-go
③	Furansu	Furansu-jin	Furansu-go
④	Doitsu	Doitsu-jin	Doitsu-go
⑤	Supein	Supein-jin	Supein-go
⑥	Ejiputo	Ejiputo-jin	Arabia-go
⑦	Kanada	Kanada-jin	Ei-go/Furansu-go
⑧	Amerika	Amerika-jin	Ei-go
⑨	Burajiru	Burajiru-jin	Porutogaru-go
⑩	Nyū-jīrando	Nyū-jīrando-jin	Ei-go
⑪	Ōsutoraria	Ōsutoraria-jin	Ei-go
⑫	Chūgoku	Chūgoku-jin	Chūgoku-go
⑬	So-ren	Roshia-jin	Roshia-go

UNIT 2
To MODIFY Things

● Key Structures

1. watashi no ie: anata no jidōsha
2. kirei-na kawa ya shizuka-na mori
3. taka·i yama to naga·i kawa
4. watashi no atarashi·i jidōsha
5. kono hito; sono hito; ano hito

---

1 $\boxed{\text{N}_1 \textbf{ no } \text{N}_2}$ N₂ of N₁

Modifying words precede the word modified. Japanese has no preposi-
tions but does have Postpositions. Therefore 'A of B' is expressed as 'B
no A.' Yet this no can be used more widely than the English 'of.'
For example, 'a book in English' and 'a book on English' are both
expressed as Ei-go no hon. Pronouns 'my,' 'your ⟨sing.⟩,' 'our,' and 'your
⟨pl.⟩' are, respectively, watashi no, anata no, watashi-tachi no, and
anata-gata no.

2 $\boxed{\text{Na N}}$ & $\boxed{\text{A·i N}}$

There are two kinds of Adjectives: Adjectives ending with -na ⟨Na⟩
and Adjectives ending with ·i ⟨A·i⟩.

3 $\boxed{\textbf{kono N; sono N; ano N}}$ this N; that N; that N

In modifying Nouns, kore, sore, and are take the forms kono, sono,
and ano. Kono/sono/ano hito may mean 'he' or 'she.' Kono/sono/ano
hito-tachi is 'they.'

New Words For UNIT 2

aka·i	red
	Cf. aka red color
ano...	that... →KS & U-15 FS
atarashi·i	new
beruto	←belt
bōshi	hat, cap
burōchi	←brooch
chiisa·i	small, little
desu	am, is, are →U-3
dochira	where?; which one?; who? →U-15 FS
-en	...yen ⟨Japanese currency⟩
furu·i	old ⟨of things, not people or animals⟩ Cf. toshi o totta/toshi-yori no old ⟨of people⟩
Ginza	⟨shopping district in Tokyo⟩

hankachi	←handkerchief
heya	room
hito	man, person
hon	book
hoteru	←hotel
ie	house
ikura	how much/many etc.? →U-4 FS
jidōsha	automobile, car
Jon	←John
kaisha	company

kasa	umbrella
kawa	river
kirei-na	clean; beautiful
kōgai	suburbs
kokki	national flag
kono...	this... →KS & U-15 FS
kuni	nation; (one's home) country
kutsu	shoes
megane	glasses
mori	forest
naga·i	long
namae	name
nekutai	←necktie
nimotsu	baggage, load
...no	of... →KS & FS
ōki·i	big, large
pasupōto	←passport
ribon	←ribbon
sebiro	(man's) suit, jacket
sen	thousand →U-6 FS
sētā	←sweater
sha·chō	president ⟨of a company⟩ →U-27 LL
shizuka-na	quiet
sono...	that... →KS & U-15 FS
sukāto	←skirt
sutokkingu	←stockings
sūtsu	←suit
sūtsu-kēsu	←suitcase
taka·i	high, tall; expensive
takushī	←taxi
tekisuto	←text
tokei	clock; watch
...wa	→U-3 KS & U-19 KS, FS
wain	←wine
yama	mountain, hill
zubon	⟨←French *jupon*⟩ trousers

1. my house : your car
2. the clean river, the quiet forest, and…
3. the high mountain and the long river
4. my new car
5. this person; that person; that person

★More Examples For Practice

1 watashi **no** jidōsha

anata **no** pen

Amerika **no** kokki

watashi-tachi **no** kaisha

kōgai **no** ie

Furansu **no** wain

Nippon-go **no** tekisuto

2 **atarashi·i** jidōsha

kirei-na kawa

shizuka-na heya

watashi no **atarashi·i** pen

watashi-tachi no **furu·i** ie

ōki·i tsukue to **chiisa·i** isu

watashi no kaisha no **atarashi·i** sha-chō

3 **kono** hon

sono pen

ano yama

ano taka·i biru

watashi no **kono** furu·i ie

---

1 my car
your pen
national flag of the US
our company
houses in the suburbs
French wine
Japanese text
2 new car
clean river
quiet room
my new pen
our old house
big desk and little chair
new president of my company
3 this book
that pen
that mountain
that tall building
this old house of mine

● Further Study

I. →Unit 2 ③ & Unit 1 ⑤ & FS

	This one etc.	This N etc.
Near the speaker	**kore**	**kono** N
Near the listener	**sore**	**sono** N
Away from both	**are**	**ano** N

II. Usual word order for modification

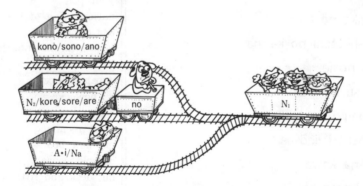

If all of these cars are coupled in order, then the phrase may become 'N₂ no kono A·i N₁,' such as watashi no kono atarashi·i jidōsha. Leaving one or more cars out does not change the order of the remaining cars.

Kore/sore/are+no means 'of this/that' and can be used like the English 'its.'

III. Omission of the modified Noun

In the phrase 'N₁ no N₂,' N₂ can be omitted when it's already understood by the listener. Watashi no, anata no, etc. mean 'mine,' 'yours,' etc. 'Na/A·i no' is used to mean 'the...one.' e.g. ōki·i no ⟨the big one⟩.

●Conversation

NAMAE WA?————————《From Airport to Hotel》

Pasupōto wa?

—Kore.

Namae wa?

—Jon Sumisu.

Kuni wa?

—Amerika.

Nimotsu wa?

—Kore to ano aka·i sūtsu-kēsu.

Ano ōki·i sūtsu-kēsu?

—Hai.

      *   *   *

—Takushī?

Are desu.

—Dōmo.

      *   *   *

Dochira?

—Ginza no Nippon Hoteru.

      *   *   *

—Kono hoteru?

Hai.

—Ikura?

Sen-en. Dōmo.

Your passport, please.
—Here it is.
Your name?
—John Smith.
Nationality?
— The United States.
Your luggage?
—This, and that red suitcase.
That big one there?
—Yes.

      *   *   *

—Taxi?
Over there.
—Thanks.

      *   *   *

Where to?
—Nippon Hotel on the Ginza.

      *   *   *

—This hotel?
Yes, sir.
—How much?
1,000 yen. Thanks.

NB: Although this conversation is an example of 'broken Japanese,' it does illustrate that you can 'get by' with only this very basic command of the language.

●Look & Learn

Things You Wear Or Carry

bōshi

ribon

megane

nekutai

hankachi

burōchi

sētā

beruto

sūtsu/sebiro

tokei

sukāto

sutokkingu

zubon

sūtsu-kēsu

kasa

kutsu

New Words For UNIT 3

arimasu	exist ⟨Inanimate⟩ →KS
asoko	⟨N⟩ (over) there
	→KS & U-15 FS
baggu	←bag
basu	←bath
benri-na	useful, convenient
chika-tetsu	subway
chizu	map
daiku	carpenter
denwa	⟨Nv⟩ telephone
depāto	←department store
desu	am, is, are →KS
dōbutsu-en	zoo
	dōbutsu animal
	-en garden
Dōzo.	⟨Cph⟩ Please, (come in).;
	Here it is.
Fuji-san	Mt. Fuji ⟨3,776 m⟩
	⟨-san here is not the -san
	meaning Mr., Ms., etc.⟩
...ga	→KS & U-19 KS & FS
ga-ka	painter
gakusei	student Cf. seito pupil
haizara	ashtray
hangā	←hanger
hiro·i	wide; spacious
imasu	exist ⟨Animate⟩ →KS
-in	⟨Suffix⟩ member of...
Irasshaimase.	⟨Cph⟩ Welcome.; Can I
	help you? ⟨phrase used
	by shop clerks⟩
isha	(medical) doctor
junsa	policeman (=keikan)
-ka	⟨Suffix⟩ -er/-or/-ist
kaisha-in	company employee
kamera	←camera
kangofu	nurse
keikan	policeman (=junsa)
kenchiku-ka	architect

	kenchiku ⟨Nv⟩ architecture
kī	←key
kōban	police box
	Cf. keisatsu(-sho) police
	station
kokku	←cook ⟨N⟩
koko	⟨N⟩ this place, here
	→KS & U-15 FS
Kōkyo	Imperial Palace
kōmu-in	public servant
	kōmu public service
...mo	...also →KS & U-19 FS
...ne.	..., isn't it? →U-27 FS
...ni	at/in [Place] →KS
omo·i	heavy
ongaku-ka	musician
	ongaku music
panda	←panda
seiji-ka	statesman, politician
	seiji politics
sensei	teacher, master
shōsetsu	novel
-shu	⟨Suffix⟩ -er/-or/-ist
soko	⟨N⟩ that place, there
	→KS & U-15 FS
suchuwādesu	←stewardess
surippa	←slippers
tawā	←tower
terebi	←television
Tōkyō	⟨capital of Japan⟩
	→U-17 LL
Ueno	⟨place name in Tokyo⟩
unten-shu	driver, chauffeur
	unten ⟨Nv⟩ driving
...wa	→KS & U-19 KS & FS
yasu·i	cheap, inexpensive
yūmei-na	famous, well-known

UNIT 3
To Describe HOW/WHAT Things ARE

● Key Structures

1. Watashi wa Amerika-jin desu.

2. Fuji-san wa kirei desu.

3. Kono heya wa hiro·i desu.

4. Koko ni hon ga arimasu.

5. Asoko ni Nippon-jin ga imasu.

6. Anata mo Amerika-jin desu.

---

1 | **N₁ wa N₂/N(a) desu.** | N₁ is N₂/Na.

Japanese has no Conjugation of Number or Person.

N(a) indicates an Na stem—an Na with the -na removed.   Compare this with 'Na modifying N.' ⟨Unit 2 ②⟩ ➡FS

2 | **N wa A·i desu.** | N is A.

3 | **[Place] ni N ga arimasu/imasu.** | There's an N in/at [Place].

When N is inanimate, arimasu is used.

When N is animate, imasu is used. ➡FS

4 | **koko/soko/asoko + ni** | in this/that place

Places near/around the speaker, near the listener, and away from both are, respectively, expressed as koko, soko, and asoko. Since these are Nouns, ni must be added to mean 'here' etc. ➡FS

5 | **N mo** | N also ➡Unit 19 FS

1. I am an American.

2. Mt. Fuji is beautiful.

3. This room is big.

4. There is a book here.

5. There is a Japanese there.

6. You are an American, too.

★More Examples For Practice

1 Watashi **wa** Sumisu **desu**.

　Ano hito **wa** Nippon-jin **desu**.

　Kore **wa** Tōkyō no chizu **desu**.

　Are **wa** watashi no atarashi·i jidōsha **desu**.

　Kono heya **wa** shizuka **desu**.

　Kono shōsetsu **wa** yūmei **desu**.

　Tōkyō no chika-tetsu **wa** benri **desu**.

2 Kono kamera **wa** yasu·i **desu**.

　Ano terebi **wa** taka·i **desu**.

　Kono baggu **wa** omo·i **desu**.

3 Ginza **ni** ōki·i depāto **ga arimasu**.

　Ueno Dōbutsu-en **ni** panda **ga imasu**.

4 **Koko ni** kasa ga arimasu.

　Asoko ni kōban ga arimasu.

　Soko ni keikan ga imasu.

5 Kono kamera **mo** yasu·i desu.

　Kore **mo** yasu·i kamera desu.

1 I'm Smith.　=My name is Smith.

That person there is Japanese.

This is a map of Tokyo.

That's my new car.

This room is quiet.

This novel is famous.

The Tokyo subways are convenient.

2 This camera is inexpensive.

That TV set is expensive.

This bag is heavy.

3 There're some big department stores in Ginza.

There are pandas in the Ueno Zoo.

4 There's an umbrella here.

There's a police box over there.

There's a policeman there.

5 This camera is cheap, too.

This is also a cheap camera.

● Further Study

I. Compare the following patterns.

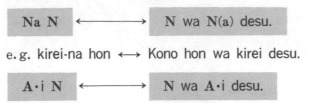

e.g. kirei-na hon ⟷ Kono hon wa kirei desu.

e.g. atarashi·i hon⟷Kono hon wa atarashi·i desu.

II. Compare arimasu with imasu.

III.   ➡Unit 1 ⑤, Unit 2 ③, & Unit 3 ④

	This one	This N	This place
Near the speaker	**kore**	**kono** N	**koko**
Near the listener	**sore**	**sono** N	**soko**
Away from both	**are**	**ano** N	**asoko**

● Conversation

IRASSHAIMASE. ————————— 《The Hotel Room》

Irasshaimase.

—Watashi wa Amerika no
   Jon Sumisu desu.

* * *

Anata no heya wa koko desu.
Dōzo.

—Hiro·i heya desu ne.
   Basu wa?

Koko desu.

—Denwa wa?

Asoko ni arimasu.

Haizara wa koko ni arimasu.

Kore wa surippa desu.

—Hangā wa?

Soko ni arimasu.

* * *

—Are wa?

Are wa Kōkyo desu.

—Kirei desu ne. Are wa?

Tōkyō Tawā desu.

* * *

Kore wa kono heya no kī desu.

—Dōmo arigatō.

Welcome.
—I'm John Smith from the
   States.
* * *
This is your room, sir.
Please (go in).
—Quite spacious, isn't it?
   Where is the bath?
Here.
—And, the telephone?
It's over there.
The ashtray is here.
These are slippers.
—Where are the hangers?
There they are.
* * *
—What's that?
That's the Imperial Palace.
—Pretty, isn't it?
   And, that?
That's Tokyo Tower.
* * *
This is your room key.
—Thank you.

● Look & Learn

What Is He/She?

gakusei	sensei	kaisha-in
daiku	isha	kōmu-in
kenchiku-ka	kangofu	ga-ka
keikan/junsa	unten-shu	ongaku-ka
suchuwādesu	kokku	seiji-ka

New Words For UNIT 4

Ā..., Oh, Yes, Well
biyōin beauty parlor
byōin hospital
chika underground
Cf. chika-tetsu subway
daitōryō president ⟨of a nation⟩
dare who? →KS & FS
deshō ka? ⟨Polite form of desu ka?⟩
donata who? ⟨Polite⟩ →FS
e painting, drawing, picture
furonto ←front desk ⟨of a hotel⟩
ginkō bank
gozaimasu ⟨Polite form of arimasu⟩
hana-ya flower shop
hana flower
-ya shop
heiwa peace
i·i good →p. 47 yo·i
...ka? →KS
kamera-ya camera shop
karu·i light ⟨not heavy⟩
Keiko ⟨female name: In many cases, Japanese women's names end with -ko. e.g. Yoshiko, Kazuko, Yōko, Hiroko, Akiko, Masako⟩
keisatsu(-sho) police station
kissaten tea shop, coffee house
kyōkai church
nan(i) what? →KS & FS
niku-ya butcher (shop)
niku meat
o- ⟨Prefix to make N/Na honorific. e.g. o-hana flower; o-kuni your country; o-namae your name⟩
onna female
onna no hito woman
Ōta ⟨family name⟩

pan ⟨←Portuguese *pão*⟩ bread
resutoran ←restaurant
sakana-ya fish shop, fishmonger
sakana fish
sarada ←salad
shōbō-sho fire station, firehouse
Cf. shōbō-jidōsha fire engine

Sore-kara, And then, After that
sūpā ←supermarket
sutēki ←steak
toire ←toilet
-ya ...shop, shop keeper
e.g. sakana-ya fish shop, fishmonger
yakkyoku pharmacy, chemist's
yao-ya vegetable shop, greengrocer
yasai-sarada vegetable salad
yasai vegetable
yūbin-kyoku post office

UNIT 4
To Ask A QUESTION

● Key Structures

1. Kore wa hon desu ka?
2. Kore wa nan desu ka?
3. Ano hito wa dare desu ka?
4. Are wa dare no jidōsha desu ka?
5. Sore wa nan no hon desu ka?

---

1 | ... ka? |

When you want to ask a question, simply put ka? at the end of the sentence. This applies for both WH-Questions and Yes/No-Questions. Unit 7 ④ tells how to answer with 'Yes' and 'No.'

2 | nan(i) ... ? | what?

Before d, t, and n sounds, nani becomes nan.

3 | dare ... ? | who?

4 | dare/donata no N? | whose N?

5 | nan no N? | what (kind of) N?

As has already been explained in Unit 2 ①, no has a broader meaning than the English 'of.' Thus, 'nan no N' can also be used when you want to get an explanation concerning N.

e.g. To the question, "Kore wa nan no hon desu ka?", you can answer, "Kore wa Ei-go no hon desu."

1. Is this a book?
2. What is this?
3. Who is that person?
4. Whose car is that?
5. What book is that?

★More Examples For Practice

1 Are wa anata no jidōsha desu **ka?**

Sono baggu wa karu·i desu **ka?**

Kono biru ni toire ga arimasu **ka?**

2 Are wa **nan** desu **ka?**

—Are wa hoteru desu.

Kono biru wa **nan** desu **ka?**

—Kore wa ginkō desu.

3 Ano onna no hito wa **dare** desu **ka?**

—Ano hito wa Ōta Keiko-san desu.

Amerika no Daitōryō wa **dare** desu **ka?**

4 Kore wa **dare no** kasa desu **ka?**

—Sore wa watashi no (kasa) desu.

Kono kasa wa **dare no** desu **ka?**

—Sore wa Ōta-san no desu.

5 Sore wa **nan no** tekisuto desu **ka?**

—Kore wa Nippon-go no tekisuto desu.

Kore wa **nan no** e desu **ka?**

—Kore wa 'Heiwa' no e desu.

---

1 Is that your car?
Is that bag light?
Is there a toilet in this building?
2 What is that?
—That's a hotel.
What is this building?
—It's a bank.
3 Who is that lady?
—She is Miss Keiko Ota.
Who's the President of the US?
4 Whose umbrella is this?
—It's mine.
Whose is this umbrella?
—That's Miss Ota's.
5 What textbook is this?
 This is a Japanese textbook.
What is this picture about?
—This is the picture *Peace*.

●Further Study

Interrogatives

I. Interrogative Pronouns

dare/donata	who?	
dochira	what direction/who?	⟨➡Unit 15 FS⟩
doko	where/what place?	⟨➡Unit 5 ④⟩
dore	which one?	⟨➡Unit 15 FS⟩
ikura	how many/much/tall/far/long etc.?	
ikutsu	how many things?	
itsu	when?	
nan(i)	what?	⟨➡Unit 4 ② & ⑤⟩
nan-gai	what floor?	⟨Cf. Unit 6 FS⟩
nan-kai	how many times?	⟨Cf. Unit 17 FS Ⅲ⟩
nan-nin	how many people?	⟨Cf. Unit 6 FS⟩

nan-ji/-nichi/-yō(bi)/-gatsu/-nen   what hour/day of the month/
day of the week/month/year?

NB: Since these are Pronouns, they may be followed by Postpositions. But, itsu and some other Interrogatives of 'time' are not followed by ni ⟨➡Unit 6 ① & ②⟩. Interrogatives asking for Number should be used in the same way as Numbers ⟨➡Unit 28 FS⟩.

II. Interrogative Adverbs and Adjective

naze	why?	⟨➡Unit 28 ①⟩
dō	how?	⟨➡Unit 15 FS⟩
donna	like what?	⟨➡Unit 15 FS⟩

NB: Interrogatives can be used as Indefinites meaning 'any~/~ever,' or 'some~' if you put -demo or -ka after them. e.g. dare-demo ⟨anyone⟩, dare-ka ⟨someone⟩, doko-demo ⟨wherever⟩, doko-ka ⟨somewhere⟩.

●Conversation

NAN NO SARADA?—— 《At the Hotel Restaurant》

—Furonto desu ka?

Hai, furonto desu.

—Kono hoteru ni resutoran ga arimasu ka?

Hai, chika ni gozaimasu.

—Arigatō.

* * *

—Sutēki ga arimasu ka?

Hai, gozaimasu.

—Sore-kara, sarada ga arimasu ka?

Hai. Nan no sarada deshō ka?

—Nan no?

Yasai sarada deshō ka?

—Hai, yasai-sarada desu.

Sore-kara, pan.

Hai.

—Sore-kara, i·i wain ga arimasu ka?

Hai, gozaimasu.

* * *

Kore wa donata no o-bōshi deshō ka?

Anata no (o-bōshi) desu ka?

—Hai, watashi no desu.

Arigatō.

—Is this the front desk?
  〈on the phone〉
Yes, sir.
—Is there a restaurant in this hotel?
Yes, there's one in the basement.
—Thanks.

* * *

—Do you have steak?
Yes, we do.
—And do you have salads?
Yes, sir. What kind of salad do you want?
—What kind?
Would that be a vegetable salad?
—Yes, a vegetable salad.
  And bread.
Yes, sir.
—And then, do you have a good wine?
Yes, we do.

* * *

Whose hat is this?
Yours?
—Yes, it's mine.
  Thank you.

●Look & Learn

My Town

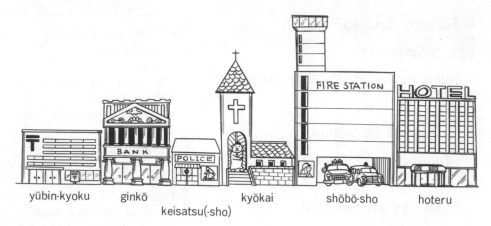

yūbin-kyoku   ginkō   kyōkai   shōbō-sho   hoteru
                         keisatsu(-sho)

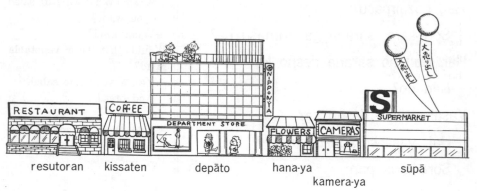

resutoran   kissaten   depāto   hana-ya   sūpā
                                                        kamera-ya

sakana-ya   yao-ya   niku-ya   biyōin   byōin   yakkyoku

New Words For UNIT 5

aki	autumn, fall	Kyōto	⟨old capital of Japan⟩
Asakusa	⟨place name in Tokyo⟩		→U-17 LL
beddo	←bed	...made	to/till...
benchi	←bench	mado	window
bōi	←boy; waiter, bellboy	mae	front, this side
bōru-pen	←ball-point pen	mannenhitsu	fountain pen
bōto	←boat	matchi	←match
chika·i	near →p. 161 ō·i	migi	⟨N⟩ right
doa	←door	mukō	the other/opposite side
doko	⟨N⟩ what place, where?	naka	⟨N⟩ inside
	→KS & U-4 FS & U-15 FS	...ni	toward/to [Place] →KS
dōro	road, street	Nikkō	⟨place name⟩ →U-17 LL
...e	to/toward [Place] →KS	nōto	←notebook
eki	station	ofisu	←office
erebētā	←elevator	Ōsaka	⟨second largest city in
-gawa	...side		Japan⟩ →U-17 LL
hana	flower, blossom	otoko	male
hashi	bridge		otoko no ko boy
hidari	⟨N⟩ left	pātī	←party
hondana	bookshelf	rai-	⟨Prefix⟩ next...
ikimasu	go	rai-nen	next year
Jē-tī-bī	←JTB ⟨Japan Travel Bu-	rai-shū	next week
	reau⟩	raitā	←lighter
jitensha	bicycle	-san	→p. 47 -san
kabin	flower vase	shita	⟨N⟩ lower part, bottom
kaerimasu	return, come/go back	soto	⟨N⟩ outside
...kara	from...	sutereo	←stereo
karendā	←calendar	taipuraitā	←typewriter
kāten	←curtain	tēburu	←table
ki	tree; wood	tō·i	far away →p. 161 ō·i
kimasu	come	tokkyū	express ⟨train⟩
-kiro	...kilometer/kilogram	tonari	⟨N⟩ next (to something)
ko	=kodomo	ue	⟨N⟩ upper part, top
	onna no ko girl	ushiro	⟨N⟩ back, the other side
kochira	this one/side/direction/	...yo.	..., I assure you. →U-27 FS
	person →U-15 FS	yoko	⟨N⟩ side
kodomo	child	Yokohama	⟨place name⟩ →U-17 LL
kōen	park		
kotae	⟨N⟩ answer		

tabako	⟨←Portuguese *tobaco*⟩
	cigarette, tobacco

UNIT 5
To Describe POSITION

● Key Structures

1. Ki no shita ni jitensha ga arimasu.

2. Watashi wa ginkō e ikimasu.

3. Watashi wa Tōkyō kara Ōsaka made ikimasu.

4. Tōkyō Eki wa doko desu ka?

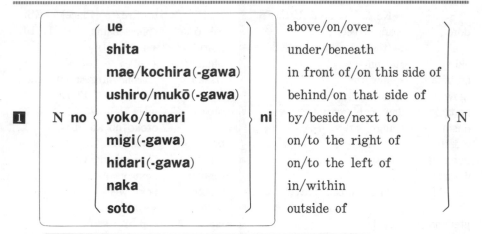

1 N no
ue	above/on/over
shita	under/beneath
mae/kochira(-gawa)	in front of/on this side of
ushiro/mukō(-gawa)	behind/on that side of
yoko/tonari	by/beside/next to
migi(-gawa)	on/to the right of
hidari(-gawa)	on/to the left of
naka	in/within
soto	outside of
ni N

2 **N wa [Place] e/ni ikimasu/kimasu/kaerimasu.**

N goes/comes/returns to [Place].

To indicate Direction, **e/ni** can be used as 'to, toward' in English. E and **ni** are interchangeable.

3 **X kara Y made**   from X to Y

4 **doko...?**   what place?

Doko is an Interrogative Pronoun and so **e**, **ni**, etc. must be used to make Adverbials like 'where.'

1. There is a bicycle under the tree.

2. I go to the bank.

3. I go from Tokyo to Osaka.

4. Where is Tokyo Station?

★More Examples For Practice

1 Hashi **no ue ni** jitensha ga arimasu.

Kōen **no naka ni** benchi ga arimasu.

Yūbin-kyoku **no migi(-gawa) ni** kaisha ga arimasu.

Yūbin-kyoku **no hidari(-gawa) ni** ginkō ga arimasu.

Ki **no shita ni** otoko no ko ga imasu.

Benchi **no ushiro ni** inu ga imasu.

2 Rai-nen watashi wa Nippon **e ikimasu**.

Anata wa pātī **ni kimasu** ka?

Rai-shū watashi wa kuni **ni kaerimasu**.

3 "Yokohama **kara** Kyōto **made**."

X **kara** Y **made**, 500-kiro desu.

X **kara** Y **made**, 5,000-en desu.

4 Koko wa **doko** desu **ka?**

—Koko wa Ginza desu.

Toire wa **doko** desu **ka?**

—Erebētā no yoko desu.

---

1 There's a bicycle on the bridge.
There's a bench in the park.
There's a company to the right of the post office.
There's a bank to the left of the post office.
There's a boy under the tree.
There's a dog behind the bench.

2 Next year I'll go to Japan.
Are you coming to the party?
Next week I'll go home (to my country).

3 "From Yokohama to Kyoto." ⟨Buying a ticket at the station/travel agency⟩
It's 500 km from X to Y.
It costs 5,000 yen (to go) from X to Y.

4 Where am I?
—This is Ginza.
Where is the toilet?
—It's by the elevator.

● Further Study

Hashi no ue ni kodomo-tachi
Hashi no shita ni bōto
Kaisha no mae ni kōban
Ki no ushiro ni onna no ko
Kawa no kochira-gawa ni kōen ⎱ ga ⎰ arimasu.
Kawa no mukō-gawa ni dōro ⎰ imasu.
Ginkō no migi ni yūbin-kyoku
Kōen no naka ni benchi
Kōen no soto ni kawa

◆ Answer the following questions about the above picture.

　　1.　Doko ni jitensha ga arimasu ka?

　　2.　Doko ni benchi ga arimasu ka?

　　3.　Doko ni kaisha ga arimasu ka?

　　4.　Doko ni inu ga imasu ka?

The answers to the above questions are hidden somewhere in this Unit.

"Doko ni kotae ga arimasu ka?"

●Conversation

HOTERU NO NAKA NI.... 《At the Travel Agency》

—Bōi-san, kono hoteru no naka ni
　Jē-tī-bī no ofisu ga arimasu ka?
Hai, gozaimasu.
—Doko desu ka?
Ano erebētā no migi-gawa desu.

＊　＊　＊

—Watashi wa Nikkō e ikimasu.
Aki no Nikkō wa kirei desu yo.
—Tōkyō kara Nikkō made tokkyū ga
　arimasu ka?
Hai, gozaimasu.
—Eki wa doko desu ka?
Asakusa desu.
Koko ni Tōkyō no chizu ga arimasu.
Kono hoteru wa koko, Asakusa wa koko
desu.
—Tō·i desu ka?
Iie, chika·i desu yo.
Kyō ikimasu ka?
—Iie, asu ikimasu.

—Bellboy! Is there a JTB
　office in this hotel?
Yes, there is.
—Where is it?
To the right of that elevator.
＊　＊　＊
—I want to go to Nikko.
Nikko is beautiful in autumn.
—Is there an express train
　from Tokyo to Nikko?
Yes, there is.
—What station does it leave
　from?
Asakusa.
Here is a map of Tokyo.
This hotel is here, and Asa-
kusa is here.
—Is it far?
No, it is near.
Are you going today?
—No, tomorrow.

▼A tourist bureau

●Look & Learn

My Room

New Words For UNIT 6

asa	morning
chotto	a little
	Chotto matte kudasai.
	⟨Cph⟩ Wait a moment.
chūsha-jō	parking lot
	chūsha ⟨Nv⟩ parking
denki-sutando	desk lamp
	denki electricity
	sutando ←stand
gakkō	school
genki	⟨N/N(a)⟩ health, vigor
go-ji	five o'clock →FS
go-kai	5th floor →FS
...goro	about [Time]
hachi-ji	eight o'clock →FS
haru	spring ⟨season⟩
hima	⟨N/N(a)⟩ free time
hiru-yasumi	noon recess
	hiru daytime, noon
	yasumi rest, day off
hōseki	jewel
ichi-ji	one o'clock →FS
ik-kai	1st floor →FS
ima	⟨N/Adv⟩ now, the present
irasshaimasu	⟨Honorific⟩ (=imasu/
	kimasu/ikimasu)
itsu	when?
-ji	...o'clock →FS
-jō	place of...
jū-ji	ten o'clock →FS
jū-ni-ji	twelve o'clock →FS
kaban	bag; briefcase
-kai	...floor →FS
kashi	=o-kashi
kon-ya	tonight (=kon-ban)
kōto	←coat
kudamono	fruit
ku-ji	nine o'clock →FS
mai-	⟨Prefix⟩ every [Time]

	→U-17 FS
mai-asa	every morning
Moshi-moshi,	⟨Cph⟩ Hello, ⟨telephone
	or speaking to somebody
	you don't know⟩
nan-ji	what time?
...ni	at/in/on [Time] →KS
ni-kai	2nd floor →FS
niku	meat, flesh
-nin	...persons →FS
o-genki	⟨N/N(a)⟩ =genki
	O-genki desu ka? ⟨Cph⟩
	How are you? ⟨To reply,
	you say "Hai, genki desu.
	Arigatō." Never say, "Hai,
	o-genki desu."⟩
o-hima	⟨N/N(a)⟩ =hima
o-kashi	sweets, candy
o-kuni	your/his/etc. country
rai-getsu	next month
rajio	←radio
reizōko	refrigerator
roku-ji	six o'clock →FS
sakana	fish
san-gai	3rd floor →FS
san-ji	three o'clock →FS
shitagi	underwear
sokkusu	←socks
Soshite,	And,
Sui-yō(bi)	Wednesday
supōtsu	←sport
supotsu-yōhin	sporting goods
	-yōhin things for...
tebukuro	gloves
uriba	counter, shop
Yā,	Hi!
yasai	vegetable
yasumi	rest, day off
yon-kai	4th floor →FS

UNIT 6
To Indicate TIME

● Key Structures

1. Anata wa itsu Nippon e ikimasu ka?
   —Kono haru (Nippon e) ikimasu.
2. Tanaka-san wa itsu ie ni kaerimasu ka?
   —Roku-ji ni (ie ni) kaerimasu.
3. Watashi wa asu san-ji goro ni koko e kimasu.

---

1 | **N wa itsu [Place] e/ni ikimasu/kimasu/kaerimasu ka?** |

When does N go/come/return to [Place]?

The word meaning 'when...?' is itsu. Look at this sentence construction. The subject comes first, then the phrase meaning time, then place, and lastly the Verb. Quite different from the English word order, isn't it? In addition, you have more freedom in Japanese so far as word order is concerned ⟨➡Unit 28 FS⟩. The only rule you have to be careful of is to put V or **desu** at the end. The rest is up to you.

Moreover, the place, or even the subject, can be omitted when it is understood by the listener. e.g. Itsu kimasu ka?

2 | **[Time] (goro) ni** | in (about) [Time]

The Postposition for Time is ni. 'At six,' 'in 1978,' and 'on Sunday': all are ...ni. Easy, isn't it? Nouns meaning Time, the four seasons, days of the week, etc. can be used as Adverbs as they are.

Put Cardinal Numbers before -ji to get '...o'clock.' ➡FS

1. When are you going to Japan?

   —I go (to Japan) this spring.

2. When does Mr. Tanaka get home?

   —He'll be back at six.

3. I'll come here about three tomorrow.

★More Examples For Practice

① Amerika no Daitōryō wa **itsu** Nippon e ikimasu **ka?**

   —Rai-nen ikimasu.

   Furansu no Daitōryō wa **itsu** Amerika ni kimasu **ka?**

   —Rai-getsu kimasu.

   Itsu kuni ni kaerimasu **ka?**

   —Rai-shū kaerimasu.

   Itsu Ōsaka e ikimasu **ka?**

   —Asu no asa ikimasu.

② Anata wa nan-ji **ni** pātī ni kimasu ka?

   —Hachi-ji **goro ni** kimasu.

   Asu no asa ku-ji **ni** gakkō e ikimasu.

   Watashi wa mai-asa jū-ji **ni** kaisha e ikimasu. Soshite, go-ji **ni** ie ni kaerimasu.

   Jū-ni-ji kara ichi-ji made, hiru-yasumi desu.

① When will the US President go to Japan?
—He'll go next year.
When will the President of France come to the States?
—He'll come next month.
When will you go home (to your country)?
—Next week.
When are you going to Osaka?
—Tomorrow morning.
② What time are you coming to the party?
—I'll come around eight.
I'll go to school at nine tomorrow morning.
I go to work at ten every morning. And I come home at five.
The noon break is from 12:00 to 1:00.

● Further Study

Numerals and the Counting Systems

♦ Japanese has many Counter Suffixes. These are only some of the more common ones.

	Cardinal Number	Things	Persons -nin	o'clock -ji	Floors -kai
1	ichi	hitotsu	hitori	ichi-ji	ik-kai
2	ni	futatsu	futari	ni-ji	ni-kai
3	san	mittsu	san-nin	san-ji	san-gai
4	shi / yon	yottsu	yo-nin	yo-ji	yon-kai
5	go	itsutsu	go-nin	go-ji	go-kai
6	roku	muttsu	roku-nin	roku-ji	rok-kai
7	shichi / nana	nanatsu	shichi-nin / nana-nin	shichi-ji / nana-ji	shichi-kai / nana-kai
8	hachi	yattsu	hachi-nin	hachi-ji	hachi-kai / hak-kai
9	ku / kyū	kokonotsu	ku-nin / kyū-nin	ku-ji	kyū-kai
10	jū	tō	jū-nin	jū-ji	jik-kai / juk-kai
11	jū-ichi	jū-ichi	jū-ichi-nin	jū-ichi-ji	jū-ik-kai
12	jū-ni	jū-ni	jū-ni-nin	jū-ni-ji	jū-ni-kai
13	jū-san	jū-san	jū-san-nin		jū-san-gai
14	jū-shi / jū-yon	jū-shi / jū-yon	jū-yo-nin		jū-yon-kai
15	jū-go	jū-go	jū-go-nin		jū-go-kai
16	jū-roku	jū-roku	jū-roku-nin		jū-rok-kai
17	jū-shichi / jū-nana	jū-shichi / jū-nana	jū-shichi-nin / jū-nana-nin		jū-shichi-kai / jū-nana-kai
18	ju-hachi	jū-hachi	jū-hachi-nin		jū-hachi-kai / jū-hak-kai
19	jū-ku / jū-kyū	jū-ku / jū-kyū	jū-kyū-nin / jū-ku-nin		jū-kyū-kai
20	ni-jū	ni-jū	ni-jū-nin		ni-jik-kai / ni-juk-kai

21	ni-jū-ichi
22	ni-jū-ni
24	ni-jū-shi/ni-jū-yon
30	san-jū
34	san-jū-shi/san-jū-yon
36	san-jū-roku
40	yon-jū/shi-jū
50	go-jū
60	roku-jū
70	nana-jū/shichi-jū
80	hachi-jū
90	kyū-jū
99	kyū-jū-kyū/kyū-jū-ku
100	hyaku
162	hyaku-roku-jū-ni
200	ni-hyaku
300	san-byaku
400	yon-hyaku
500	go-hyaku
600	rop-pyaku
700	nana-hyaku
800	hap-pyaku
900	kyū-hyaku
1,000	sen
1,976	sen-kyū-hyaku-nana-jū-roku
2,000	ni-sen
3,000	san-zen
4,000	yon-sen
5,000	go-sen
6,000	roku-sen
7,000	nana-sen
8,000	has-sen
9,000	kyū-sen
10,000	ichi-man

●Conversation

O-HIMA DESU KA?————————《Calling A Friend》

—Moshi-moshi, Tanaka-san desu ka?

Watashi wa Amerika no Jon Sumisu

desu.

Kaoru-san, irasshaimasu ka?

Hai, chotto matte kudasai.

* * *

Yā, Jon-san desu ka?

Ima doko ni imasu ka?

—Nippon Hoteru ni imasu.

O-genki desu ka?

—Arigatō, genki desu.

Anata wa kon-ya o-hima desu ka?

Iie, pātī ga arimasu.

Asu wa o-hima desu ka?

—Iie, watashi wa asu Nikkō e ikimasu.

Itsu kaerimasu ka?

—Sui-yōbi no san-ji goro, hoteru ni

kaerimasu.

—Hello, Mr. Tanaka?
  This is John Smith from the States.
  Is Kaoru there?
Yes. Wait a moment, please.

* * *

Hi, is that you, John?
Where are you now?
—I'm at the Nippon Hotel.
How are you?
—Fine, thank you.
  Are you free this evening?
No, I've got a party.
Are you free tomorrow?
—No, I'm going to Nikko tomorrow.
When do you get back?
—I'll be back at this hotel about three on Wednesday.

●Look & Learn

Department Store

_____ no uriba wa doko desu ka?   ⟨Where can I get _____?⟩

— _____ -kai desu.   ⟨—On the _____ floor.⟩

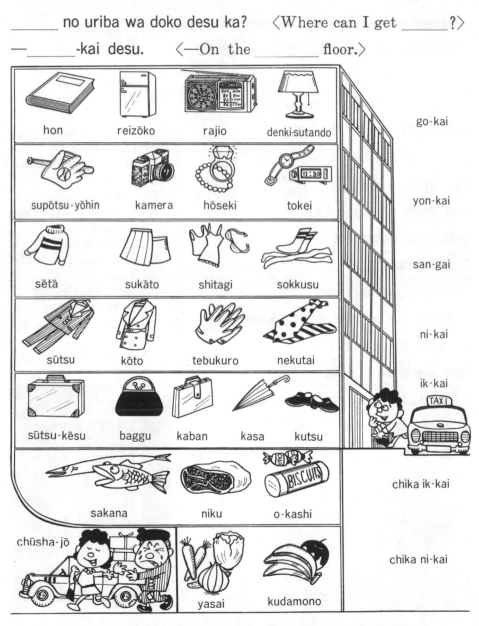

| | | | | go-kai |
| hon | reizōko | rajio | denki-sutando | |

| | | | | yon-kai |
| supōtsu-yōhin | kamera | hōseki | tokei | |

| | | | | san-gai |
| sētā | sukāto | shitagi | sokkusu | |

| | | | | ni-kai |
| sūtsu | kōto | tebukuro | nekutai | |

| | | | | | ik-kai |
| sūtsu-kēsu | baggu | kaban | kasa | kutsu | |

| | | | chika ik-kai |
| sakana | niku | o-kashi | |

chūsha-jō

| | | | chika ni-kai |
| | yasai | kudamono | |

New Words For UNIT 7

arimasen	do not exist ⟨Inanimate⟩ →KS
dewa arimasen	not be →KS
-gatsu	⟨Counter Suffix for names of the months of the year⟩ →FS
ikimasen	not go →KS
jinja	Shinto shrine

Kingu-kongu	←King Kong
machi	town, city; street
mon	gate
-nichi	⟨Counter Suffix for days⟩ →FS
oishi·i	delicious
onii-san	older brother →LL
o-tera	=tera

otōto	younger brother →LL
ringo	apple
-san	⟨To express intimacy or friendliness, we sometimes put -san after a Noun.⟩ e.g. oji-san dear uncle, sakana-ya-san fishmonger
shuto	capital city
sō	so →U-15 FS Sō desu. ⟨Cph⟩ It's so., That's right.
tera	Buddhist temple
tomodachi	friend
Tōshōgū	⟨famous shrine at Nikko⟩

-yō(bi)	⟨Suffix for names of the days of the week⟩
yo·i	good ⟨i·i is good, yoku-na·i is not good, yo·katta was good ⟨→U-10⟩, yoku-na·katta was not good ⟨→U-10⟩⟩
Yōmei Mon	⟨famous gate of Toshogu at Nikko⟩

UNIT 7
To Be NEGATIVE

● Key Structures

1. Watashi wa sensei dewa arimasen.

2. Kono machi wa shizuka dewa arimasen.

3. Kono ringo wa oishi·ku-na·i desu.

4. Ano hito wa Tōkyō e ikimasen.

5. Anata wa Amerika-jin desu ka?

   —Iie, sō dewa arimasen.

---

1 | N₁ **wa** N₂/N(a) **dewa arimasen.** | N₁ is not N₂/Na.

2 | N **wa** A·ku-na·i desu. | N is not A.

Here, and later, A indicates the stem of A·i. The only exception is yo· for i·i ⟨good⟩.

3 | V·masu→V·masen |

So far, we've learned five Verbs—arimasu, imasu, ikimasu, kimasu, and kaerimasu—all ending with ~masu. Negative forms for these are made by changing ~masu into ~masen and replacing 'N ga' with 'N wa.' ➔Unit 19 **3**

4 | Hai, sō desu. | & | Iie, sō dewa arimasen. |

We learned in Unit 4 how to make Questions, by putting ka? at the end of the statement. When the answer is either "Yes," or "No," you can answer using the above Constructions if the question is in the ... desu ka? form and using Hai, V·masu or Iie, V·masen if the question is in the ...V·masu ka? form.

1. I am not a teacher.

2. This town is not quiet.

3. This apple is not delicious.

4. That person does not go to Tokyo.

5. Are you an American?

   —No, I am not.

★More Examples For Practice

1 Watashi wa kaisha-in **dewa arimasen**.

Ano hito wa kenchiku-ka **dewa arima-sen**.

Are wa anata no hon **dewa arimasen**.

Tōkyō no kawa wa kirei **dewa arimasen**.

2 Kono reizōko wa yasu·**ku-na·i desu**.

Ano terebi wa taka·**ku-na·i desu**.

Kono baggu wa omo·**ku-na·i desu**.

3 Dōbutsu-en ni Kingu-kongu **wa imasen**.

Kyō ano hito wa ki**masen**.

4 Tōkyō wa Nippon no shuto desu ka?

—Hai, sō desu.

Anata wa Keiko-san no onii-san desu ka?

—Iie, sō dewa arimasen. Otōto desu.

Jon-san wa kyō no pātī ni kimasu ka?

—Hai, kimasu.

Anata wa asu Tōkyō e ikimasen ka?

—Hai, ikimasen.

—Iie, ikimasu.

1 I'm not a company employee.
He's not an architect.
That's not your book.
The rivers in Tokyo aren't clean.
2 This refrigerator is not cheap.
That TV set is not expensive.
This bag isn't heavy.
3 King Kong is not in the zoo.
He won't come today.
4 Is Tokyo the capital of Japan?
—Yes, it is.
Are you Keiko's older brother?
—No. I'm her younger brother.
Will John come to today's party?
—Yes, he will.
Aren't you going to Tokyo tomorrow?
—No, I'm not.
—Yes, I am.

● Further Study

Names of Times

I. Names of the Months (=Cardinal Number+gatsu)

Ichi-gatsu	Jan.	Ni-gatsu	Feb.	San-gatsu	Mar.
Shi-gatsu	Apr.	Go-gatsu	May	Roku-gatsu	June
Shichi-gatsu	July	Hachi-gatsu	Aug.	Ku-gatsu	Sept.
Jū-gatsu	Oct.	Jū-ichi-gatsu	Nov.	Jū-ni-gatsu	Dec.

II. Names of the Days of the Month

Tsuitachi	1st	Futsuka	2nd	Mikka	3rd	Yokka	4th
Itsuka	5th	Muika	6th	Nanoka	7th	Yōka	8th
Kokonoka	9th	Tōka	10th				

Jū-ichi-nichi 11th … (=Cardinal Number+nichi) … Jū-ku-nichi 19th

Hatsuka 20th Ni-jū-ichi-nichi 21st … (Cardinal Number+nichi)

… San-jū-ichi-nichi 31st

NB: The 14th and the 24th are usually called Jū-yokka and Ni-jū-yokka respectively.

III. Names of the Days of the Week

Nichi-yō(bi)	Sun.	Getsu-yō(bi)	Mon.	Ka-yō(bi)	Tues.
Sui-yō(bi)	Wed.	Moku-yō(bi)	Thurs.	Kin-yō(bi)	Fri.
Do-yō(bi)	Sat.				

Hai; Iie vs. Yes; No

The Japanese Hai; Iie do not correspond exactly to the English "Yes; No." We say "Hai" when we agree with the questioner's literal meaning/phrasing, and "Iie" when we disagree, regardless of whether the Verb in the answer is affirmative or negative. e.g. Ikimasen ka? Hai, ikimasen. Iie, ikimasu.

●Conversation

HAI, SŌ DESU.————————《Visiting Nikko》

Koko wa Tōshōgū desu.

—Kore wa o-tera desu ka?

Iie, o-tera dewa arimasen.

Jinja desu.

—Atarashi·i jinja desu ka?

Iie, atarashi·ku-na·i desu.

Kore wa yūmei-na Yōmei Mon desu.

—Kore mo furu·i desu ka?

Hai, furu·i desu.

       *   *   *

Anata wa Furansu-jin desu ka?

—Iie, sō dewa arimasen.

   Watashi wa Amerika-jin desu.

Nippon ni tomodachi ga imasu ka?

—Hai, Tōkyō ni imasu.

Amerika-jin no tomodachi desu ka?

—Iie, Nippon-jin desu.

       *   *   *

Kyō Tōkyō ni kaerimasu ka?

—Iie, kaerimasen.

   Sui-yōbi ni kaerimasu.

This is Toshogu.
—Is this a Buddhist temple?
No, it's not a temple.
It's a Shinto shrine.
—Is this a new shrine?
No, it's not new.
This is the famous Yomei-mon.
—Is this also old?
Yes, it is.

       *   *   *

Are you French?
—No, I'm not.
  I'm American.
Do you have any friends in Japan?
—Yes, I've some in Tokyo.
Are your friends American?
—No, Japanese.

       *   *   *

Are you going back to Tokyo today?
—No, I'm not.
  I'm going back on Wednesday.

▼Yomei-mon

●Look & Learn

My Family

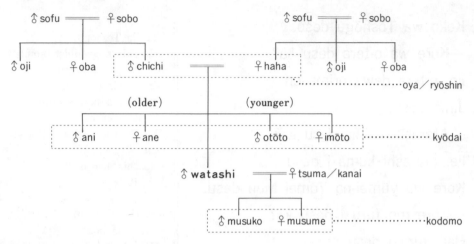

Someone Else's Family

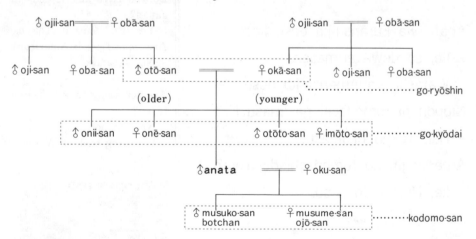

NB: When you refer to your elders, you can occasionally use the words basically indicating the second or third person's family even if they are your own relatives. e.g. Watashi no otō-san

'My husband' and 'your/her husband' are shujin and go-shujin respectively.

New Words For UNIT 8

※From now on, Verbs are introduced in their stem forms.

agar·	to rise, go up	mi·	to watch, see, look
ar·	to exist, be ⟨The V·nai	ne·	to lie down; go to bed;
	form of ar· is never used⟩		sleep
	...ga ar· There's...	nobor·	to climb; rise
aruk·	to walk	nom·	to drink
asa-gohan	breakfast		kusuri o nom· to take
	asa morning		medicine
aw·	to meet	nor·	to ride, get on
	...ni/to aw· to meet...		...ni nor· to ride (on)...
ban-gohan	supper, dinner	...o	→KS
	ban night	ochi·	to fall →LL
daigaku	college, university	oki·	to get up; rise →LL
de·	to come/go out; appear,	ore·	to break ⟨Vi⟩ →LL
	show up; leave, graduate	ori·	to climb down; get off
	...o/kara de· to come/go	rekōdo	←record
	out of..., leave...	sagar·	to fall →LL
densha	tram, train	shin·	to die
gaido-bukku	←guidebook	Shinkyō	⟨famous bridge at Nikko⟩
gohan	boiled rice; meal	Sō desu ka?	⟨Cph⟩ Is that so?;
hair·	to enter		Really?
	...ni hair· to enter...	suber·	to slip
hanas·	to speak, tell, talk	sugu	soon
hashir·	to run	sukoshi	⟨N/Adv⟩ a little, a few
i·	to exist, be, stay	suru	to do
ik·	to go	tabe·	to eat
imōto	younger sister →U-7 LL	tabun	probably
isog·	to hurry up	taihen	very
Jā,	Well, then; Bye!	taore·	to fall down →LL
kaer·	to come/go back	tat·	to stand up
kak·	to write; draw	tegami	letter, epistle
kaw·	to buy	tenki	(good) weather
kik·	to listen, hear	tob·	to jump; fly
korogar·	to roll	tomar·	to stop ⟨Vi⟩; stay
kotoshi	this year	tsuk·	to arrive
kudar·	to come down		...ni tsuk· to arrive at...
kuru	to come	ugok·	to move
magar·	to bend, turn ⟨Vi⟩	uisukī	←whiskey
mat·	to wait	Un...,	Yes..., Well,
mawar·	to spin, go round	yoku	often

UNIT 8
To Describe WHAT You Do

● Key Structures

1. Watashi wa terebi o mimasu.
2. Anata wa ban-gohan o tabemasu.
3. Imōto ni tegami o kakimasu.
4. Koko de densha o orimasu.
5. Mai-asa roku-ji ni ie o demasu.

---

1 $\boxed{\text{N o } V^{M}}$

As you know, English verbs can be classified into two categories: transitive and intransitive. A transitive verb is one followed by an object noun. Most Japanese Verbs equivalent in meaning to English transitive verbs are preceded by Nouns with o. Exceptions are; norimasu ⟨ride⟩, hairimasu ⟨enter⟩, aimasu ⟨meet⟩, and a few others which are preceded by N ni.

V^{M}, hereafter, indicates V·masu, V·masen, etc. ➡below

2 $\boxed{V^{v}; \ V^{c}; \ V^{x}}$

The V·masu form, in which the five Verbs so far have been introduced, is not, in fact, the basic form for Verbs. Accordingly, Verbs will be introduced from now on in their stem forms ⟨V⟩. You will be expected to make the V^{M} forms by yourself. Don't worry, it's not difficult to make the V^{M} forms. ➡FS

All Verbs can be grouped into three categories:

① V^{v}: Verb stems ending with vowels e or i
② V^{c}: Verb stems ending with consonants
③ V^{x}: the Irregular Verbs kuru ⟨to come⟩ and suru ⟨to do⟩

1. I watch TV.
2. You eat supper.
3. I write a letter to my younger sister.
4. I get off the tram here.
5. I leave home at six every morning.

★More Examples For Practice

1 Anata wa yoku terebi **o** mimasu ka?

—Hai, yoku mimasu.

Anata wa yoku rekōdo **o** kikimasu ka?

—Hai, yoku kikimasu.

Watashi wa mai-asa hachi-ji ni asa-gohan

o tabemasu.

Wain **o** nomimasu ka?

—Iie, uisukī **o** nomimasu.

Anata wa atarashi·i sutereo **o** kaimasu

ka?

—Hai, kaimasu.

Sumisu-san **o** machimasu ka?

Anata wa Nippon-go **o** hanashimasu ka?

—Hai, sukoshi hanashimasu.

Chūgoku-go **mo** hanashimasu ka?

—Iie, hanashimasen.

NB: N o+mo ⟨➡Unit 3 5⟩ →N mo

➡Unit 19 FS

Takushī **ni** norimasu ka?

Otōto wa kotoshi daigaku **ni** hairimasu.

1 Do you watch TV very much?
—Yes, I often watch TV.
Do you often listen to records?
—Yes, I often listen to records.
I have breakfast at eight every morning.
Do/Will you drink wine?
—No, I drink whiskey.
Are you going to buy a new stereo set?
—Yes, I am.
Will you/Shall we wait for Smith?
Do you speak Japanese?
—Yes, I speak a little.
Do you speak Chinese, too?
—No, I don't.
Will you/Shall we take a taxi?
My younger brother will start college this year.

● Further Study

How to Make V・masu Forms

I. Vᵛ ⟨Vowel-ending Verbs⟩

Final Vowels		
~e		
~i		

+ **masu**

e.g.

tabe・ → tabe**masu**

oki・ → oki**masu**

II. Vᶜ ⟨Consonant-ending Verbs⟩

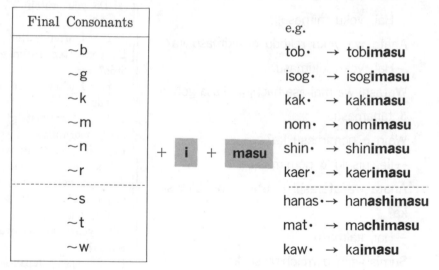

Final Consonants
~b
~g
~k
~m
~n
~r
~s
~t
~w

+ **i** + **masu**

e.g.

tob・ → tob**imasu**

isog・ → isog**imasu**

kak・ → kak**imasu**

nom・ → nom**imasu**

shin・ → shin**imasu**

kaer・ → kaer**imasu**

hanas・→ han**ashimasu**

mat・ → ma**chimasu**

kaw・ → ka**imasu**

III. Vˣ ⟨Irregular Verbs⟩

kuru ⟶ **kimasu**

suru ⟶ **shimasu**

Sound Law ⟨1⟩ s+i→ shi

t+i→ chi

w+i→ i

◆Now you can make the V・masu forms for the following Verbs, can't you?

ik・ ⟨to go⟩; kuru ⟨to come⟩; kaer・ ⟨to return⟩; tabe・ ⟨to eat⟩

ne・ ⟨to go to bed⟩; aruk・ ⟨to walk⟩; hashir・ ⟨to run⟩

hanas・ ⟨to speak⟩; ar・ ⟨to exist⟩; i・ ⟨to exist/stay⟩

●Conversation

NAN-JI NI KAERIMASU KA?———《An Appointment》

—Moshi-moshi, Kaoru-san?

　　Jon desu.

　　Ima Nikkō ni imasu.

Sō desu ka?

I·i tenki desu ka?

—Hai, taihen i·i tenki desu.

　　Ima aka·i hashi no mae ni imasu.

Shinkyō desu ne.

—Chotto matte kudasai. . . .

　　Gaido-bukku o mimasu. . . .

　　Un. . ., tabun sō desu.

Asu nan-ji ni Tōkyō e kaerimasu ka?

—Asa jū-ji ni koko no hoteru o demasu.

　　Jū-ichi-ji no tokkyū ni norimasu.

　　Ni-ji goro Tōkyō ni tsukimasu.

　　Sore-kara sugu Nippon Hoteru ni

　　kaerimasu.

Jā, watashi wa ni-ji goro kaisha o

demasu.

—Hello, Kaoru?
　This is John.
　I'm in Nikko now.
Is that so?
Are you having good weather?
—Yes, it is very nice.
　I'm in front of a red bridge.
You mean Shinkyo Bridge, don't you?
—Hold on a minute.
　I'll look at my guidebook.
　Well…, perhaps you're right.
What time will you get back to Tokyo tomorrow?
—I'll leave the hotel here at ten in the morning.
　I'll take the 11:00 express.
　I'll get to Tokyo about two, and then I'll return to my hotel immediately.
Then I'll leave my office around two.

▼Shinkyo Bridge

●Look & Learn

Basic Movements

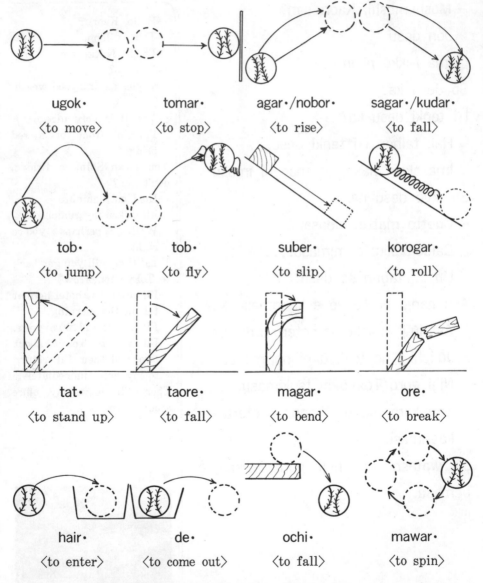

ugok·	**tomar·**	**agar·/nobor·**	**sagar·/kudar·**
⟨to move⟩	⟨to stop⟩	⟨to rise⟩	⟨to fall⟩
tob·	**tob·**	**suber·**	**korogar·**
⟨to jump⟩	⟨to fly⟩	⟨to slip⟩	⟨to roll⟩
tat·	**taore·**	**magar·**	**ore·**
⟨to stand up⟩	⟨to fall⟩	⟨to bend⟩	⟨to break⟩
hair·	**de·**	**ochi·**	**mawar·**
⟨to enter⟩	⟨to come out⟩	⟨to fall⟩	⟨to spin⟩

♦ Make the V·masu forms for the above Verbs.

New Words For UNIT 9

aruite	by walking, on foot ←aruk· →U-12 FS	or·	to bend and break →LL
asob·	to play, amuse oneself	os·	to push
basu	←bus	oso·i	late; slow
chichi	(my) father →U-7 LL	otos·	to drop 〈Vt〉
...de	① at/in [Place]	oyog·	to swim
	② with/by means of...	pūru	←(swimming) pool
eiga	movies	robī	←lobby
Fōdo	←Ford	-san	① Mr./Mrs./Miss/Ms.
fune	ship, boat		② After Nouns to express
hanas·	to let go, leave		intimacy or friendliness
hashi	chopsticks	Satō	〈family name〉
hashitte	by running ←hashir· →U-12 FS	Shinkansen	〈'bullet' super-express lines of the Japanese National Railways, soon to crisscross all of Japan〉
hik·	to pull		
hikō-ki	airplane		
hon-ya	bookstore	shokuji	〈Nv〉 meal
ire·	to let...enter; pour	Sō desu ne.	〈Cph〉 That sounds good.
isoide	in a hurry ←isog· →U-12 FS	Sore-dewa,	Well, then,
		sushi	〈Japanese cuisine; raw fish slices on vinegared rice〉
issho-ni	together		
itsu-mo	always		
Jā, mata.	〈Cph〉 See you. →p. 173 mata again	tanoshi·i	pleasant, amusing tanoshi·ku merrily, pleasantly
-ki	machine for...		
kōhī	←coffee	tenisu	←tennis
kon-ban	tonight (=kon-ya)	...to	with... →KS
kotori	(small) bird	tome·	to stop 〈Vt〉
kuruma	vehicle, automobile	tsukam·	to seize, grasp
Kyūshū	〈Southern island of Japan〉 →U-17 LL	uchi	house; my home/company
		uke·	to receive, catch
		umi	sea, ocean
mage·	to bend, turn 〈Vt〉	utaw·	to sing
mai-nichi	every day		Cf. uta song
mata	again 〈also used in parting as in "See you again." →p. 173〉		
miruku	←milk		
nage·	to throw		
natsu	summer		

UNIT 9
To Tell HOW/WHERE You Do Things

● Key Structures

1. Watashi-tachi wa Nippon e hikō-ki de ikimasu.

2. Kodomo-tachi wa kōen de tenisu o shimasu.

3. Kon-ban imōto-san to uchi e kimasu ka?

4. Kotori wa tanoshi·ku utaimasu.

5. Watashi wa kaisha e aruite ikimasu.

6. Watashi wa hoteru de tomodachi ni aimasu.

1 | [Something] **de** | with/by means of [Something]

2 | [Place] **de** | at/in [Place]

The Postposition de is used after [Place] to tell where a given action or event takes place. Don't confuse this with the ni used after [Place] ⟨➡Unit 3 ③⟩ to indicate where a given object exists or ⟨➡Unit 5 ②⟩ the direction of a given action.

3 | N **to** | together with N

4 | A·**ku**; N(a)-**ni** | Adj + ly→Adv

5 | V·**te** V^M |

V·**te** functions just like the English '~ing.' This Construction can be used in the expressions; aruite ik· ⟨to go (by) walking⟩, hashitte ik· ⟨to go (by) running⟩, isoide ik· ⟨to go (by) hurrying⟩, etc. Unit 12 FS explains how to make this V·te form.

6 The Possessive can be omitted when it is understood.

1. We go to Japan by plane.

2. Children play tennis in the park.

3. Will you come to my house with
   your sister this evening?

4. A bird sings merrily.

5. I go to work on foot.

6. I'll meet (my) friend at the hotel.

★**More Examples For Practice**

1 Watashi wa basu **de** kaisha e ikimasu.

Kyūshū e Shinkansen **de** ikimasu ka?

Nippon-jin wa hashi **de** gohan o tabemasu.

2 Anata wa itsu-mo doko **de** nemasu ka?

—Ni-kai **de** nemasu.

Anata wa natsu pūru **de** oyogimasu ka?

—Iie, umi **de** oyogimasu.

3 Mai-nichi chichi **to** tenisu o shimasu.

Sono hon-ya-san de Ōta-san **to** aimasu.

Watashi wa yoku Nippon-jin no tomodachi **to** Nippon-go de hanashimasu.

Itsu-mo dare **to** eiga o mimasu ka?

—Satō-san ya Fōdo-san **to** mimasu.

Watashi **to** ikimasu ka? Tanaka-san **to**
ikimasu ka?

—Anata **to** ikimasu.

4 Kon-ban oso·**ku** kaerimasu.

Kodomo wa soto de genki-**ni** asobimasu.

5 Soko e arui**te** ikimasu ka?

—Iie, jitensha de ikimasu.

1 I go to work by bus.
Will you go to Kyushu by
Shinkansen?
Japanese eat with chop-
sticks.
2 Where do you usually
sleep?
—I sleep upstairs.
Do you swim in the pool in
summer?
—No, I swim in the ocean.
3 I play tennis with my
father every day.
I'll meet Ota at the bookstore.
I often speak (in) Japanese
with my Japanese friends.
With whom do you usually
go to the movies?
—With Sato and Ford.
Will you go with me? Or
with Mr. Tanaka?
—I'll go with you.
4 I'll get home late tonight.
Children play outdoors cheer-
fully.
5 Are you going there on
foot?
—No, I'll go by bicycle.

● Further Study

How to Make V^M Forms

	Affirmative	Negative
Present	V·masu ➡ Unit 8 FS	V·masen ➡ Unit 7 ③
Past	V·mashita ➡ Unit 10 ②	V·masen deshita ➡ Unit 10 ④

How to Get There

hikō·ki de	densha de	kuruma/jidōsha de
jitensha de	basu de	takushī de
chika·tetsu de	fune de	Shinkansen de
aruite	hashitte	isoide

●Conversation

I·I DESU NE.————— 《Over A Cup Of Coffee》

Hoteru no robī de aimasu ka?

—Hai.

Sore-dewa, watashi wa aruite ikimasu.

—Watashi wa Asakusa kara takushī de

kaerimasu.

Isoide kaerimasu.

Jā, mata.

—Jā.

*   *   *

—Kōhī o nomimasu ka?

I·i desu ne. Doko de?

—Kono hoteru no chika ni resutoran

ga arimasu.

*   *   *

Miruku o iremasu ka?

—Hai, chotto. . ., arigatō.

*   *   *

Issho-ni shokuji o shimasen ka?

—I·i desu ne.

Sushi o tabemasu ka?

—Sō desu ne.

Shall we meet at the hotel lobby?
—Yes.
Then, I'll walk there.
—I'll go back from Asakusa by taxi.
I'll hurry.
See you then.
—See you.

*   *   *

—How about having coffee?
Good idea. But where?
—There is a restaurant in the basement of this hotel.

*   *   *

Do you put milk in (your coffee)?
—Yes, a little..., thanks.

*   *   *

Shall we have dinner together?
—Good.
Shall we have sushi?
—That sounds good.

▼Kaminari-mon in Asakusa

●Look & Learn

Basic Actions

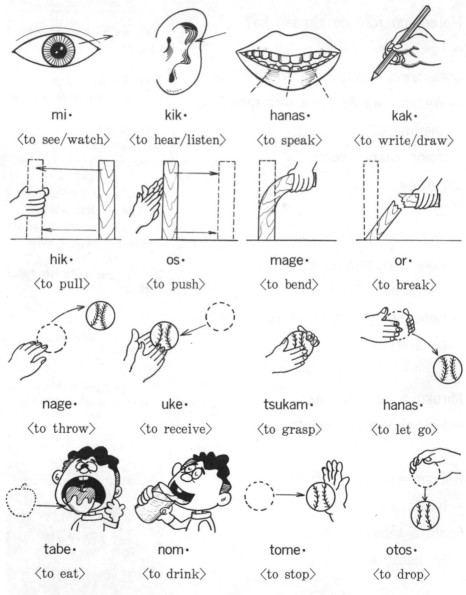

mi·
⟨to see/watch⟩

kik·
⟨to hear/listen⟩

hanas·
⟨to speak⟩

kak·
⟨to write/draw⟩

hik·
⟨to pull⟩

os·
⟨to push⟩

mage·
⟨to bend⟩

or·
⟨to break⟩

nage·
⟨to throw⟩

uke·
⟨to receive⟩

tsukam·
⟨to grasp⟩

hanas·
⟨to let go⟩

tabe·
⟨to eat⟩

nom·
⟨to drink⟩

tome·
⟨to stop⟩

otos·
⟨to drop⟩

♦ Make the V·masu forms for the above Verbs.

New Words F... UNIT 10

Afurika	←Africa
ame	⟨N⟩ rain
	ame ga fur· it rains, to rain
asatte	the day after tomorrow
ashita	tomorrow (=asu)
atataka·i	warm
atsu·i	hot
	atsu·katta was hot
	atsu·ku-na·katta was not hot
ban	night
	Cf. ban-gohan supper
Demo,	But,
deshita	was, were →KS
fuyu	winter
gaido	←(tourist) guide
gogo	⟨N/Adv⟩ afternoon, p.m.
gozen	⟨N/Adv⟩ morning, a.m.
hiru	⟨N/Adv⟩ noon; daytime
ikimashita	went ←ik·
Kegon no Taki	Kegon Falls ⟨famous waterfall at Nikko⟩

kinō	yesterday
konsāto	←concert
kumori	⟨N⟩ cloudy weather
	←kumor· to get cloudy

kyonen	last year
mirai	future
mukashi	⟨N/Adv⟩ old times, long ago
omoshiro·i	interesting; funny
ototoi	the day before yesterday
samu·i	cold ⟨only of weather⟩
	Cf. tsumeta·i cold ⟨of things you can touch, wind, and feelings⟩
setsumei	⟨Nv⟩ explanation
shashin	photo
shinsetsu-na	kind, obliging
shōrai	⟨N/Adv⟩ future
shōsetsu-ka	novelist
taki	waterfall
takusan	⟨N/Adv⟩ much; many
tanjōbi	birthday
	Watashi no tanjōbi wa jū-ni-gatsu ni-jū-yok-ka desu. ⟨My birthday is Dec. 24.⟩
tor·	to take
	shashin o tor· to take a picture
yom·	to read
yoru	⟨N/Adv⟩ night
yūbe	⟨N/Adv⟩ last night
yūgata	⟨N/Adv⟩ evening
zannen-na	regrettable
	Zannen desu ne. ⟨Cph⟩ That's too bad. ; I'm sorry to hear that.

UNIT 10
To Describe The WAY Things WERE

● Key Structures

1. Kinō wa watashi no tanjōbi deshita.
2. Kyonen watashi wa Afurika e ikimashita.
3. Kono shōsetsu-ka wa yūmei dewa arimasen deshita.
4. Ōta-san wa hoteru ni imasen deshita.
5. Ototoi wa atsu・katta desu.
6. Kinō wa atsu・ku-na・katta desu.

---

1 | N_1 **wa** N_2/N(a) **deshita.** | N_1 was N_2/Na.

2 | **N wa V・mashita.** | N did....

To express Past events, change desu, ~masu to deshita, ~mashita.

3 | N_1 **wa** N_2/N(a) **dewa arimasen deshita.** | N_1 wasn't N_2/N(a).

4 | **N wa V・masen deshita.** | N didn't....

To express Negative Past, add deshita after ~masen.

5 | **N wa A・katta desu.** | N was A.

| **N wa A・ku-na・katta desu.** | N wasn't A.

The Past form of A・ku-na・i desu is A・ku-na・katta desu, because A・ku-na・ can be treated just like any other Adjective. ➡FS

1. Yesterday was my birthday.

2. I went to Africa last year.

3. This novelist was not famous.

4. Mr. Ota was not at the hotel.

5. It was hot the day before yesterday.

6. It was not hot yesterday.

★More Examples For Practice

1 Kinō wa Nichi-yō(bi) **deshita**.

Ame **deshita**.

2 Nippon e hikō-ki de iki**mashita** ka?

—Hai, hikō-ki de iki**mashita**.

Fuji-san o mi**mashita** ka?

—Hai, mi**mashita**.

3 Kinō wa tenki **dewa arimasen deshita**.

Kumori deshita.

Kōen wa shizuka **dewa arimasen**

deshita.

Kodomo-tachi ga takusan imashita.

4 Kotoshi mo umi de oyogi**masen deshita**.

Pūru de oyogimashita.

Kinō anata wa soko e ikimashita ka?

—Iie, iki**masen deshita**.

5 Kinō wa atataka・**katta desu**.

Samu・**ku-na・katta desu**.

Yūbe no konsāto wa yo・**katta desu**.

Sono shōsetsu wa omoshiro・**katta desu**.

1 Yesterday was Sunday.
It was rainy.
2 Did you go to Japan by plane?
—Yes, I went by plane.
Did you see Mt. Fuji?
—Yes, I saw it.
3 It was not good weather yesterday.
It was cloudy.
The park was not quiet.
There were many children there.
4 I didn't swim in the ocean this year either.
I swam in a pool.
Did you go there yesterday?
—No, I didn't.
5 It was warm yesterday.
It was not cold.
The concert last night was good.
That novel was interesting.

● Further Study

How to Make Past Forms

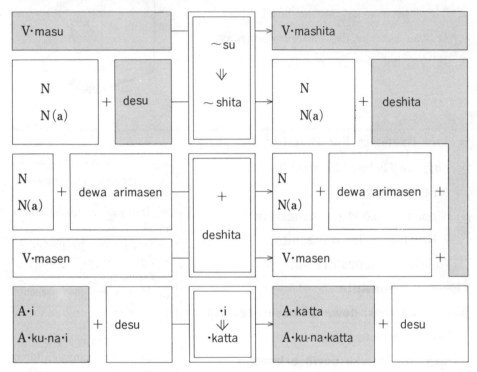

NB: A·ku·na·i, V·nai ⟨➡Unit 13 FS⟩, and V·tai ⟨➡Unit 21 FS⟩ have the same conjugational forms as A·i.

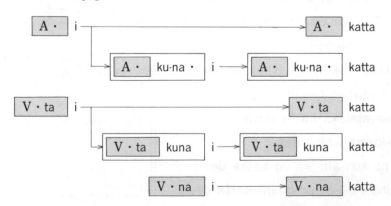

●Conversation

ZANNEN DESU NE.————《Talking About Travel》

Nikkō wa samu·katta desu ka?

—Iie, samu·ku-na·katta desu.

  I·i tenki deshita.

  Tanoshi·katta desu.

Tōkyō wa ame deshita.

—Pātī wa tanoshi·katta desu ka?

Hai, taihen tanoshi·katta desu.

Anata no tomodachi no Emirī-san mo

kimashita yo.

—Emirī-san wa genki deshita ka?

Hai.

Nikkō de shashin o torimashita ka?

—Iie, torimasen deshita.

Kegon no Taki o mimashita ka?

—Iie, mimasen deshita.

Sō desu ka? Zannen desu ne.

Taihen yūmei-na taki desu.

Gaido wa Ei-go de setsumei-

shimashita ka?

—Iie, Nippon-go deshita.

  Demo, shinsetsu-na gaido-san

  deshita.

Was it cold at Nikko?
—No, it wasn't cold.
  The weather was good.
  I had a good time.
It rained in Tokyo.
—Did you enjoy your party?
Yes, it was a lot of fun.
Your friend Emily was also
there.
—How was Emily?
Fine. Did you take any
pictures at Nikko?
—No, I didn't.
Did you see Kegon Falls?
—No, I didn't.
Really? That's too bad.
It's a very famous waterfall.
Did your guide explain in
English?
—No, it was in Japanese.
  But she was a considerate
  guide.

▼Cedar trees in Nikko

●Look & Learn

Time Flies

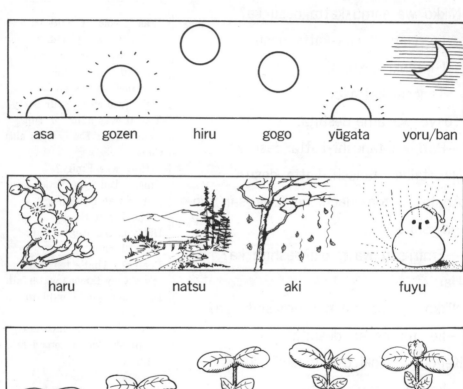

asa   gozen   hiru   gogo   yūgata   yoru/ban

haru   natsu   aki   fuyu

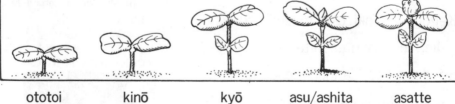

ototoi   kinō   kyō   asu/ashita   asatte

mukashi   ima   mirai/shōrai

New Words For UNIT 11

age·	to give →KS & FS
"Ai rabu yū."	←'I love you.'
apāto	←apartment, flat
bara	rose
benkyō	⟨Nv⟩ study
bifuteki	←beefsteak
epuron	←apron
esukarētā	←escalator
Gakken	⟨name of a publishing company⟩
haha	(my) mother →U-7 LL
janbo-jetto	←jumbo jet ⟨Boeing 747⟩
jī-pan	⟨←jean pants⟩ jeans
jiyū	⟨N/N(a)⟩ freedom, liberty Jiyū no Megami Statue of Liberty
kane	metal; money
kānēshon	←carnation
kure·	to give →KS & FS
maiku	←mike, microphone
megami	goddess
meron	←melon
mise	shop
miyage	souvenir, present
moraw·	to receive, get→KS & FS
naifu	←knife
...ni	from/by [Person] →KS
ningyō	doll

oba-san	aunt →U-7 LL
oji-san	uncle →U-7 LL
o-kane	money
o-miyage	=miyage
orenji	←orange
ōtobai	←autobike, motorcycle

(Courtesy of Suzuki Motor Co., Ltd.)

purezento	⟨Nv⟩ ←present
rēn-kōto	←raincoat
sandoitchi	←sandwich
supōtsu-kā	←sports car

(Courtesy of Nissan Motor Co., Ltd.)

tēpu-rekōdā	←tape recorder
wai-shatsu	←white shirt ⟨Wai-shatsu, or Y-shatsu, originally meant a 'white' shirt, but it has changed in meaning and today means a 'dress shirt'; hence we have **karā-wai-shatsu** 'color' white shirts!⟩
Yoshida	⟨family name⟩

UNIT 11
To Say GIVE Or GET

● Key Structures

1. Watashi wa oji-san kara purezento o moraimashita.
2. Watashi wa anata ni kono hon o agemasu.
3. Anata wa ano hito ni kamera o agemasu ka?
4. Anata wa watashi ni kono shashin o kuremasu ka?
5. Oba-san wa watashi ni purezento o kuremashita.

---

1 [Person^X] **wa** [Person^Y] **kara/ni** [Something] **o moraw·**

[Person^X] receives/gets [Something] from [Person^Y].

2 [Person^X] **wa** [Person^Y] **ni** [Something] **o age·**

[Person^X] gives [Something] to [Person^Y].

3 [Person^X] **wa** [Person^Y] **ni** [Something] **o kure·**

[Person^X] gives [Something] to [Person^Y].

There are two Verbs meaning 'to give' —age· and kure·.

The difference in usage between these depends upon the relation between the giver and the receiver. Age· is used when First Person gives to Second/Third Person, Second Person to Third Person, and Third Person to Third Person. Kure· is used in all other cases.

Moraw· means 'to receive.' This is used when First Person receives from Second/Third Person, Second from Third, and Third from Third. When Second/Third Person receives from First Person, or Third from Second, other Constructions using age· ⟨→FS⟩ are used in preference to moraw·.

1. I got a present from my uncle.

2. I'll give this book to you.

3. Are you giving a camera to that person?

4. Will you give me this photo?

5. My aunt gave me a present.

★**More Examples For Practice**

1. Watashi wa anata kara kinō o-kane o **moraimashita**.

   Watashi wa Tanaka-san kara kono hōseki o **moraimashita**.

   Anata wa tanjōbi ni oba-san kara nani o **moraimashita** ka?

   Amerika wa Furansu kara 'Jiyū no Megami' o **moraimashita**.

2. (Watashi wa) anata ni kono hon o **agemasu**.

   Watashi wa haha ni kānēshon o **agemashita**.

   (Anata wa) sono bara o dare ni **agemasu** ka?

3. (Anata wa) watashi ni kono e o **kuremasu** ka?

   —Hai, agemasu.

   Satō-san wa watashi ni tegami o **kuremashita**.

1. I got money from you yesterday.
   I got these jewels from Mr. Tanaka.
   What did you get from your aunt on your birthday?
   America got the Statue of Liberty from France.

2. I'll give this book to you.
   I gave my mother a carnation.
   Whom will you give that rose to?

3. Are you giving me this picture?
   —Yes, it's for you.
   Mr. Sato wrote me a letter.

● Further Study

Give and Get—— age·, kure·, and moraw·

Age· originally meant 'to give upward (to)', with kure· the opposite, meaning 'to give downward (to).' So age· is used when the lower person gives to the higher person and kure· when the higher gives to the lower.

Third Person is regarded as the highest, First Person as the lowest, and Second Person in the middle. This ranking of Persons is based on the First Person's closeness to the other Persons, those persons who are closer

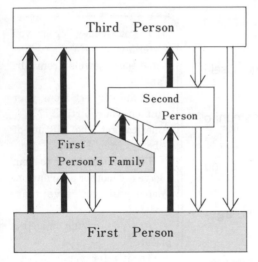

being regarded as lower. Therefore, a Third Person who is very close to the First Person—such as a member of the First Person's family—is lower than an ordinary Second Person.

The use of moraw· is restricted to those cases when the relationship between the giver and the receiver is the same as with kure·.

→: age·, ⇒:kure·, moraw·

◆Choose the correct Verbs meaning 'give.'

			Answers
Watashi wa anata ni			①
Watashi wa Jon-san ni			①
Anata wa watashi ni		① agemasu.	②
Anata wa Jon-san ni	purezento o		①
Jon-san wa watashi ni		② kuremasu.	②
Jon-san wa anata ni			②
Chichi wa Jon-san ni			①

●Conversation

TAIHEN I·I HON DESU. ─────────── 《A Present》

—Kore wa Nikkō no o-miyage desu.

Dōmo arigatō.

Nan desu ka?

—Ningyō desu. Ano aka·i hashi no

mae no mise de kaimashita.

* * *

—Kirei-na nekutai desu ne.

Kore desu ka? Pātī de Emirī-san

kara moraimashita.

Watashi wa Emirī-san ni Nippon-go no

hon o agemashita.

—Emirī-san mo Nippon-go o benkyō-

shimasu ka?

Hai.

—Sore wa i·i hon desu ka?

Hai, taihen i·i hon desu.

Gakken no Nippon-go no tekisuto

desu.

—Ā, are desu ka?

Watashi mo moraimashita.

Yoshida-san kara moraimashita.

—This is a present from
   Nikko.
Thank you.
What is it?
—A doll. I bought this at
   the shop in front of that
   red bridge.

* * *

—That's a beautiful tie.
This? Emily gave it to me at
the party.
I gave her a book on the
Japanese language.
—Oh, is Emily studying
   Japanese, too?
Yes.
—Is it a good book?
Yes, it's a very good book.
It's a Japanese textbook
published by Gakken.
—Oh, that book. I've got one,
   too.
   Mr. Yoshida gave me a
   copy.

▼A Japanese textbook

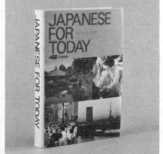

●Look & Learn

Guess What... Familiar Names, Perhaps...?

kamera
purezento
rajio
terebi
sutereo
supōtsu-kā
erebētā
esukarētā
naifu
meron
orenji
kōhī
sandoitchi
ōtobai
wai-shatsu
bifuteki
tēpu-rekōdā
janbo-jetto
toire
apāto
depāto
maiku
jī-pan
epuron
rēn-kōto
"Ai rabu yū."

New Words For UNIT 12

ake·	to open ⟨Vt⟩
	Cf. ak· to open ⟨Vi⟩
chūi	⟨Nv⟩ attention, caution
...de	→KS
deguchi	exit, way out
fuirumu	←film
hijō-guchi	emergency exit
hiru-gohan	lunch
	hiru daytime, noon
hitotsu	one →U-6 FS
ijime·	to bully, treat harshly,
	be cruel to, tease
ikimashō	let's go
	←ik· →KS
iriguchi	entrance
-kata	how to... →U-18 FS
kēki	←cake
kiken-na	dangerous
kin'en	No Smoking
kippu	ticket
kudasai	please give →KS
man	ten thousand →U-6 FS
mina-san	everybody
mise·	to show
mite	←mi· →KS & FS
noriba	(bus) stop, (train) platform
odor·	to dance
oshie·	to teach, tell
o-te-arai	toilet (=toire)
Pīsu	←Peace ⟨brand of Japanese cigarettes⟩
renzu	←lens
Sā,	Now,; Well,
sawag·	to make noise, be rowdy
	Cf. sawagashi·i noisy
sawar·	to touch
serufu-taimā	←self-timer ⟨on a camera⟩
shattā	←shutter ⟨on a camera;

	for a door⟩
shibafu	turf, lawn
sō	so →U-15 FS
	Sō desu. ⟨Cph⟩ It's so.; That's right.
	Sō desu ka? ⟨Cph⟩ Is that so?; Really?
	Sō desu ne. ⟨Cph⟩ That sounds good.
	Sō shimashō. ⟨Cph⟩ Let's.; That's a good idea.
	Sō, sō. ⟨Cph⟩ Oh, yes!
Sumimasen.	⟨Cph⟩ Sorry.; Excuse me.
suw·	to inhale
	tabako o suw· to smoke
	suwanai do not smoke
suwar·	to sit down
tabemashō	let's eat ←tabe· →KS
takushī-noriba	cabstand
tsukai-kata	how to use, usage
	←tsukaw· →U-18 FS
tsukaw·	to use
waraw·	to laugh; smile
yukkuri	slowly, without haste

▼Pīsu

UNIT 12
To Make A REQUEST Or An INVITATION

● **Key Structures**

1. Kore o kudasai.

2. Kore o mite kudasai.

3. Koko de tabako o suwanai de kudasai.

4. Issho-ni ikimashō.

5. Issho-ni hiru-gohan o tabemashō ka?

---

1 | **N o kudasai.** | Please give me N.

2 | **V・te kudasai.** | Please do. . . .

As seen in Unit 9 **5**, V・te functions like the English '～ing' form. V・te kudasai literally means, 'Please give me (your) ～ing,' which can easily mean, 'Please do... (for me/us).'

V・te by itself can be used for making requests in conversation among friends. e.g. "Chotto matte!" ⟨Wait a moment!⟩ ➡FS

3 | **V・nai de kudasai.** | Please don't. . . .

Unit 13 FS explains how to make these V・nai forms.

As with V・te, V・nai de can also be used alone to indicate a negative request in friendly conversation. e.g. "Ikanai de!" ⟨Don't leave me.⟩

4 | **V・mashō** | Let's do. . . ./I will do. . . .

The V・mashō form is made by changing ～masu to ～mashō.

5 | **V・mashō ka?** | Shall we/I do. . . ?

1. Give me this, please. (I'll take this.)

2. Look at this, please.

3. Please do not smoke here.

4. Let's go together.

5. Shall we have lunch together?

★**More Examples For Practice**

1 Kōhī to kēki **o kudasai**.

   'Pīsu' **o** hitotsu **kudasai**.

2 Chotto mat**te kudasai**.

   Ei-go de hanashi**te kudasai**.

   Yukkuri hanashi**te kudasai**.

   Sono rajio o mise**te kudasai**.

3 Shashin o tora**nai de kudasai**.

   Koko de sawaga**nai de kudasai**.

   Nippon no mina-san, inu o ijime**nai de kudasai**.

4 Sā, iki**mashō**.

   Issho-ni utai**mashō**.

5 Odori**mashō ka?**

   —Odorimashō.

   Kono eiga o mi**mashō ka?**

   —Hai, mimashō/sō shimashō.

   Kono shashin o age**mashō ka?**

   —Hai, kudasai.

   Mado o ake**mashō ka?**

   —Hai, akete kudasai.

1 Give me coffee and cake.
One pack of 'Peace,' please.
2 Wait a moment, please.
Please speak in English.
Will you speak slowly?
Show me that radio.
3 Don't take pictures.
Don't be noisy here.
People of Japan, please
don't be cruel to dogs.
4 Let's go.
Let's sing together.
5 Shall we dance?
—Yes, let's (dance).
Shall we watch this movie?
—Yes, let's.
Shall I give you this photo?
—Yes, please (give it to me).
Shall I open the window?
—Yes, please (open it).

● Further Study

How to Make V・te Forms

I.   V^v 〈Vowel-ending Verbs〉

Final Vowels
~e
~i

+ **te** ⟶

~ete
~ite

e.g.

tabe・→ tabe**te**

oki・ → oki**te**

II.   V^c 〈Consonant-ending Verbs〉

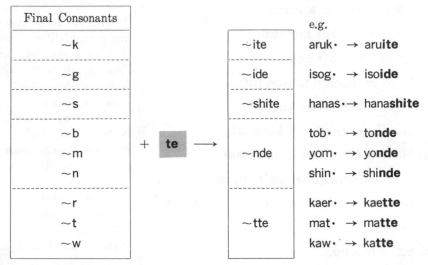

Final Consonants
~k
~g
~s
~b
~m
~n
~r
~t
~w

+ **te** ⟶

~ite
~ide
~shite
~nde
~tte

e.g.

aruk・ → arui**te**

isog・ → isoi**de**

hanas・→ hana**shite**

tob・ → to**nde**

yom・ → yo**nde**

shin・ → shi**nde**

kaer・ → kae**tte**

mat・ → ma**tte**

kaw・ → ka**tte**

NB: ik・〈to go〉→ **itte** 〈not iite〉

III.   V^x 〈Irregular Verbs〉

kuru ⟶ **kite**

suru ⟶ **shite**

◆Change the following useful Verbs into their V・te forms, which can be used to express simple and friendly requests: "V・te!"

① ik・〈to go〉 ② kuru・〈to come〉 ③ kaer・〈to go/come back〉 ④ hair・〈to go/come in〉 ⑤ oki・〈to get up〉 ⑥ waraw・〈to smile/laugh〉 ⑦ suwar・〈to sit down〉 ⑧ mat・〈to wait〉 ⑨ ake・〈to open〉 ⑩ suru・〈to do〉

●Conversation

OSHIETE KUDASAI. ——— 《Buying A Camera》

—I·i kamera-ya-san o oshiete
kudasai.

Kamera o kaimasu ka?

Jā, issho-ni ikimashō.

* * *

Irasshaimase.

—Kono kamera o misete kudasai.

Kore desu ka?   Dōzo.

—Chotto omo·i desu ne.

Sumimasen. Renzu ni sawaranai

de kudasai.

—Sumimasen.   Tsukai-kata o oshiete
kudasai.

Kore wa shattā desu.

Serufu-taimā wa kore desu.

* * *

—Kono kamera o kudasai.

Ikura desu ka?

Roku-man-go-sen-en desu.

Fuirumu o iremashō ka?

—Hai, irete kudasai.

—Do you know a good camera
shop?
Are you going to buy a
camera?
In that case, let's go together.

* * *

Can I help you?
—Will you show me this
camera?
This one? Please.
—A little heavy, isn't it?
Excuse me, but please don't
touch the lens.
—Sorry. Tell me how to use
this, will you?
This is the shutter.
The self-timer is here.

* * *

—I'll take this camera.
How much?
65,000 yen. Shall I put film
in it for you?
—Yes, please.

▼A camera shop

●Look & Learn

Attention!

Iriguchi
⟨ Entrance ⟩

Deguchi
⟨ Exit ⟩

Hijō-guchi
⟨ Emergency Exit ⟩

Shibafu ni hairanai de kudasai.
⟨ Keep off the grass ⟩

Chūi
⟨ Caution ⟩

Kiken
⟨ Danger ⟩

Kin'en
⟨ No Smoking ⟩

Yūbin-kyoku
⟨ Post Office ⟩

Denwa
⟨ Telephone ⟩

Takushī-noriba
⟨ Cabstand ⟩

Kippu
⟨ Tickets ⟩

O-te-arai
⟨ Toilet ⟩

Answers to the questions on page 80

① Itte!　② Kite!　③ Kaette!　④ Haitte!　⑤ Okite!　⑥ Waratte!

⑦ Suwatte!　⑧ Matte!　⑨ Akete!　⑩ Shite!

New Words For UNIT 13

Ā,	Hey!, You!, Oh!
aka-chan	baby
akirame·	to give up, despair
chūnen	middle age
Ē,	Yes,; Sure,
ganbar·	to do one's best, persevere
hatarak·	to work, labor
ikanakereba	if...do not go ←ik· →KS
ike·	can go/be all right ikemasen is not all right; is not good →KS
kawanakute	not buying ←kaw· →KS
kekkon	⟨Nv⟩ marriage

koi	⟨Nv⟩ love ⟨between man and woman⟩ Cf. ai love ⟨in general⟩ koibito lover
misenakute	not showing ←mise· →KS
mō	now, already
mochiron	of course
nar·	to bear fruit Cf. p. 167 narimasen is not fruitful; is not good →KS
nayam·	to worry; suffer
nug·	to take off, undress ⟨Vi⟩
ōki-ku nar·	to grow up/larger

otona	grown-up person Cf. kodomo child
rikon	⟨Nv⟩ divorce
rōjin	old person
saikon	⟨Nv⟩ remarriage
seichō	⟨Nv⟩ growing, growth
seinen	youth, young man
shitsuren	⟨Nv⟩ unrequited love, heartbreak
shōjo	girl
shōnen	boy
taishoku	⟨Nv⟩ retiring from work, leaving a company
tor·	to take; bring [Something] shashin o tor· to take a picture toshi o tor· to get old
toshi	(person's) age; year Anata (no toshi) wa ikutsu desu ka? = Anata wa nan-sai desu ka? How old are you?
toshi-yori	aged person
umare·	to be born
wakamono	youth, young people
yangu	←young, youth

UNIT 13
To PERMIT, PROHIBIT, Or DEMAND

● Key Structures

1. Soko e itte mo i·i desu.

2. Koko de tabako o sutte wa ikemasen.

3. Pasupōto o misenakute mo i·i desu.

4. Kippu o kawanakute wa ikemasen.

5. Ku-ji made ni ofisu e ikanakereba narimasen.

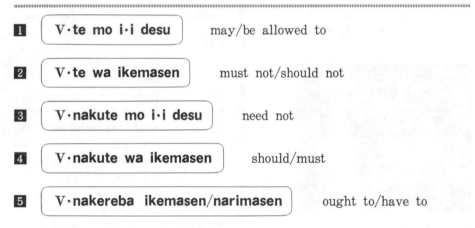

1 | V·te mo i·i desu | may/be allowed to

2 | V·te wa ikemasen | must not/should not

3 | V·nakute mo i·i desu | need not

4 | V·nakute wa ikemasen | should/must

5 | V·nakereba ikemasen/narimasen | ought to/have to

As you remember, V·te functions just like the English '~ing.' If you don't remember, →Unit 9 ⑤ & Unit 12 ②. In Construction ①, i·i desu means 'is good,' so, for example, Itte ⟨ik· 'to go'⟩ mo i·i desu literally means, 'Going is also good,' which easily translates as permission to go.

In Construction ②, ikemasen means 'is not good,' and so Itte wa ikemasen literally means, 'Going is not good,' or 'You mustn't go.' Note, however, that even though ikemasen may logically seem to be the Negative of ikemasu, this ikemasu is never used in place of i·i desu in Construction ① & ③.

The V·nakute, V·nakereba forms are derived from V·nai. →FS

1. You can go there.

2. You shouldn't smoke here.

3. You don't need to show your passport.

4. You must buy a ticket.

5. I have to go to the office by nine.

★More Examples For Practice

1 Anata wa mō kaet**te mo i·i desu**.

Koko de tabako o sut**te mo i·i desu** ka?

—Hai, **i·i desu**.

2 Koko ni hait**te wa ikemasen**.

Kodomo wa kono hon o yon**de wa ikemasen**.

3 Ashita ko**nakute mo i·i desu**.

Kutsu o nuga**nakute mo i·i desu** ka?

4 Anata wa isoide ika**nakute wa ikemasen**.

Kutsu o nuga**nakute wa ikemasen** ka?

5 Nippon-go de hanasa**nakereba narimasen** ka?

—Hai, Nippon-go de hanashite kudasai.

Ei-go de hanashite wa ikemasen.

—Iie, Nippon-go de hanasanakute mo i·i desu.

Ei-go de hanashite mo i·i desu.

Yukkuri hanashite kudasai.

1 You may go (back) now.
May I smoke here?
—Yes, you may.

2 You shouldn't come in here.
Children mustn't read this book.

3 You don't have to come tomorrow.
Don't I have to take off my shoes?

4 You must hurry.
Do I have to take off my shoes?

5 Must I speak in Japanese?
—Yes, please speak in Japanese.
You shouldn't speak in English.
—No, you need not speak in Japanese.
You may speak in English.
Speak slowly, please.

●Further Study

How to Make V•nai Forms

I. V^v ⟨Vowel-ending Verbs⟩

$$V^v + \boxed{\textbf{nai}}$$

e.g. tabe•→ tabe**nai**

oki• → oki**nai**

II. V^c ⟨Consonant-ending Verbs⟩

$$V^c + \boxed{\textbf{a}} + \boxed{\textbf{nai}}$$

e.g. kak• → kak**anai**

yom•→ yom**anai**

shin•→ shin**anai**

kaw•→ kaw**anai**

III. V^x ⟨Irregular Verbs⟩

kuru ⟶ **konai**

suru ⟶ **shinai**

NB: (1) Aranai, which can be deduced as the V•nai form of ar• ⟨to exist⟩, is never used ⟨Cf. arimasu; arimasen⟩. The proper negation is simply na•i.

(2) V•nakute, V•nakereba, and V•nakatta ⟨V^p Past Negative; →Unit 10 FS & Unit 14 FS⟩ are derived from V•nai by changing ~i of V•nai into ~kute, ~kereba, and ~katta respectively, just as you would do with an ordinary A•i.

Choose the proper answers to the questions.

① Itte mo i•i desu ka?

② Itte wa ikemasen ka?

③ Ikanakute mo i•i desu ka?

④ Ikanakute wa ikemasen ka?

⑤ Ikanakute wa narimasen ka?

ⓐ Iie, itte mo i•i desu.

ⓑ Iie, itte wa ikemasen.

ⓒ Iie, ikanakute mo i•i desu.

ⓓ Iie, ikanakute wa ikemasen.

ⓔ Iie, ikanakereba narimasen.

Answers: ①-ⓑ; ②-ⓐ; ③-ⓓ, ⓔ; ④-ⓒ; ⑤-ⓒ

●Conversation

MOSHI-MOSHI,———《Visiting The Imperial Palace》

—Koko wa Kōkyo desu ka?

Ē, sō desu.

—Iriguchi wa doko desu ka?

Takusan arimasu.

Are mo sō desu.

—Haitte mo i·i desu ka?

Mochiron i·i desu.

        ＊   ＊   ＊

—Shashin o totte mo i·i desu ka?

I·i desu.

        ＊   ＊   ＊

Moshi-moshi, koko de tabako o sutte wa ikemasen.

—Sumimasen.

        ＊   ＊   ＊

—Bōshi o nuganakute wa ikemasen ka?

Iie, nuganakute mo i·i desu.

        ＊   ＊   ＊

Ā, moshi-moshi, shibafu ni haitte wa ikemasen.

—Is this the Imperial Palace?

Yes, it is.

—Where is the entrance?

There are many entrances.

That's one of them.

—May I go in?

Of course, you may.

       ＊   ＊   ＊

—May I take pictures?

You may.

     ＊   ＊ ＊

Hey, you! You're not allowed to smoke here.

—Sorry.

       ＊   ＊   ＊

—Should I take off my hat?

No, you don't need to.

       ＊   ＊   ＊

Hey, keep off the grass.

▼Kōkyo

●Look & Learn

This Is Life.

Age

shin· ⟨to die⟩

?

70 → rōjin/toshi-yori
⟨old person⟩

60 ↑

toshi o tor· ⟨to get old⟩
taishoku-suru ⟨to retire⟩
akirame· ⟨to give up⟩

50 ↑

ganbar· ⟨to do one's best⟩

chūnen
⟨middle-aged person⟩

otona
⟨grown-up⟩

40 ↑

hatarak· ⟨to work⟩

saikon-suru ⟨to remarry⟩
rikon-suru ⟨to get divorced⟩
kekkon-suru ⟨to marry⟩

30 ↑

seinen/wakamono/
yangu ⟨youth⟩

20 ↑

nayam· ⟨to be distressed⟩
shitsuren-suru
　⟨to be heartbroken⟩
koi o suru ⟨to fall in love⟩

shōnen ⟨boy⟩
shōjo ⟨girl⟩

10 ↑

ōkiku nar·/seichō-suru
　⟨to grow⟩

kodomo ⟨child⟩

0 aka-chan ⟨baby⟩

umare· ⟨to be born⟩

New Words For UNIT 14

ato-kara	afterwards, later	mō sukoshi	a little more/longer
byōki	⟨N⟩ illness, disease		
chigaina·i	not different	mō ichi-nen	another year
	...ni chigaina·i surely... →KS	...nochi	...later →U-29 FS
da	→KS & U-23 FS	o-isha-san	=isha
daiyamondo	←diamond	oku-san	his/your/etc. wife →U-7 LL
Dari	←Dali, Salvador ⟨Spanish painter, 1904– ⟩	omoidas·	to recollect, remember
denwa ga ar·	to get a telephone call	...rashi·i	apparently, obviously →KS
deshō	will/may be, probably →KS	Sā?...	Well,; Let me see....
Dewa,	Now,; Then,	shire·	can be sure ⟨This can not be used in the Affirmative⟩
fuk·	to blow		shiremasen cannot be sure, cannot know for sure
fur·	to fall ⟨rain, snow, etc.⟩		Cf. shirimasen I don't know
	ame ga fur· to rain		...kamo shiremasen maybe..., can possibly... →KS
	yuki ga fur· to snow		
hare	⟨N⟩ fine/clear weather	...sō	it's said... →KS
hare·	to clear up ⟨weather⟩	suzushi·i	cool ⟨only of weather⟩
haretari, kumottari	Sometimes clear, sometimes cloudy.	taifū	typhoon
hazu	⟨N⟩ expectation, natural course of things →KS	tenki-yohō	weather forecast
			tenki weather
Hokkaidō	⟨Northern island of Japan⟩ →U-17 LL		yohō ⟨Nv⟩ forecast
ichiji	for a short time; once Cf. ichi-ji one o'clock	tenrankai	exhibition
		tochū	⟨N⟩ midway
isogashi·i	busy		tochū de on the way, *en route*
Iya,	No,	tokidoki	sometimes
...kamo	can possibly... →KS	tsuyu	rainy season ⟨June⟩
kare	he	...yō	⟨N(a)⟩ appearance of..., manner of... →KS
	Cf. kare-ra they ⟨male/general⟩	yōji	errand, business, engagement (=yō)
kaze	wind	yuki	⟨N⟩ snow
	kaze ga fuk· it blows, to blow ⟨Vi⟩		yuki ga fur· it snows, to snow
kumor·	to get cloudy Cf. kumori cloudy weather		
mō...	more/another...		

UNIT 14
To Hazard A GUESS

TAPE ②-Ⓐ

● Key Structures

1. Ano hito wa o-isha-san kamo shiremasen.
2. Ashita mo ame deshō.
3. Yoshida-san wa kuru hazu desu.
4. Kore wa daiyamondo ni chigaina·i desu.
5. Yoshida-san wa mō kaetta yō desu.
6. Ano hito-tachi wa kekkon-suru rashi·i desu.
7. Ōsaka no chika-tetsu wa benri da sō desu.

---

1 | N/N(a)/A·i/Vᴾ **kamo shiremasen** | ⟨maybe⟩

2 | N/N(a)/A·i/Vᴾ **deshō** | ⟨probably⟩

3 | N no/Na/A·i/Vᴾ **hazu desu** | ⟨naturally expected⟩

4 | N/N(a)/A·i/Vᴾ **ni chigaina·i desu** | ⟨surely⟩

The degree of certainty is lowest with ①, and highest with ④.
Vᴾ indicates the Plain forms of Verbs. ➡FS

5 | N no/Na/A·i/Vᴾ **yō desu** | ⟨seemingly⟩

This is used for guesses based mainly upon observation.

6 | N/N(a)/A·i/Vᴾ **rashi·i desu** | ⟨apparently⟩

7 | N da/N(a) da/A·i/Vᴾ **sō desu** | ⟨it is said⟩

This is used for statements based upon information from others.

1. That person may be a doctor.

2. It will probably rain tomorrow, too.

3. Mr. Yoshida is expected to come.

4. This must be a diamond.

5. It seems Mr. Yoshida has already gone home.

6. It looks as though they are going to get married.

7. I hear the Osaka subways are convenient.

★More Examples For Practice

1. Asu wa samu·**i kamo shiremasen**.

   Kono inu wa shin**u kamo shiremasen**.

2. Kaoru-san wa **kuru deshō**.

   Keiko-san wa **konai deshō**.

3. Ano hito wa o-isha-san **no hazu desu**.

   Dari no tenrankai wa rai-shū ar**u hazu desu**./rai-shū **no hazu desu**.

4. Ano hito wa suchuwādesu **ni chigaina·i desu**.

   Kaoru-san wa **kuru ni chigaina·i desu**.

5. Ano hito wa kangofu **no yō desu**.

   Keiko-san wa **konai yō desu**.

6. Kotoshi Hokkaidō wa atataka·**i rashi·i desu**.

   Sumisu-san wa Amerika e kaer**u rashi·i desu**.

7. Ano hito wa ongaku-ka **da sō desu**.

   Sumisu-san wa Amerika e kaer**u sō desu**.

   Hokkaidō no fuyu wa samu·**i sō desu**.

---

1. It may be cold tomorrow. This dog may die.

2. Kaoru will come, I suppose. Keiko will probably not come.

3. He must be a doctor. There is supposed to be a Dali exhibition (held) next week.

4. She is certainly a stewardess. Kaoru is sure to come.

5. She seems to be a nurse. It seems Keiko won't come.

6. It looks like Hokkaido is having a warm winter. It looks as though Mr. Smith is going to go back to the States.

7. He is said to be a musician. It is said Smith'll return to the USA. I hear winter in Hokkaido is very cold.

● **Further Study**

How to Make V^P Forms ➡Unit 23 FS

	Affirmative	Negative
Present	V·u ➡below	V·nai ➡Unit 13 FS
Past	V·ta ➡Unit 17 FS	V·nakatta ➡Unit 10 FS & Unit 13 FS

How to Make V•u Forms

I. V^v ⟨Vowel-ending Verbs⟩

$$V^v + \boxed{r} + \boxed{u}$$

e.g. tabe· → tabe**ru**

oki· → oki**ru**

II. V^c ⟨Consonant-ending Verbs⟩

$$V^c + \boxed{u}$$

e.g. kak· → kak**u**

isog· → isog**u**

hanas·→ hanas**u**

asob· → asob**u**

yom· → yom**u**

shin· → shin**u**

kaer· → kaer**u**

mat· → ma**tsu**

kaw· → ka**u**

> Sound Law ⟨2⟩
>
> t+u → tsu
>
> w+u→ u

III. V^x ⟨Irregular Verbs⟩

kuru ⟶ **kuru**

suru ⟶ **suru**

NB: These V•u forms are often called 'dictionary forms,' since Verbs are usually listed in their V•u forms in most Japanese dictionaries.

●Conversation

MACHIMASHŌ. ————————————— 《People Meet》

Emirī-san wa konai kamo shiremasen
ne.... Byōki rashi·i desu.

—Ā, sō desu ka?

 Biru-san wa kimasu ka?

Tabun kuru deshō. Oku-san to issho-
ni kuru hazu desu.

—Yoshida-san wa?

Sā?..., kuru sō desu ga....

—Satō-san mo kimasu ka?

Iya, Satō-san wa konai yō desu.

Isogashi·i rashi·i desu.

* * *

Yā, Biru-san! Oku-san wa?

—Ato-kara kimasu.

 Issho-ni ie o demashita ga, tochū
 de yōji o omoidashimashita.

Yoshida-san wa kimasu ka?

—Yoshida-san wa kuru ni chigaina·i
 desu. Yūbe kare kara denwa ga
 arimashita.

Dewa, mō sukoshi machimashō.

Emily may not come.
I hear she's ill.
—Oh, she is?
 Is Bill coming?
Probably. He is supposed to
come with his wife.
—What about Yoshida?
Well..., he's expected, but....
—Is Sato coming, too?
Apparently not.
He seems to be busy.

* * *

Hi, Bill! Where's your wife?
—She'll be along later.
 We left home together, but
 halfway here she remem-
 bered something she had
 to do.
Will Yoshida come?
—He's sure to come. I got
 a call from him last night.
Then let's wait for a while.

▼Waiting for friends

●Look & Learn

Weather Forecast

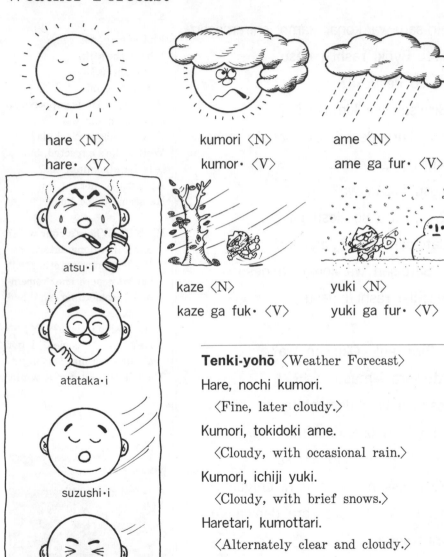

hare ⟨N⟩
hare· ⟨V⟩

kumori ⟨N⟩
kumor· ⟨V⟩

ame ⟨N⟩
ame ga fur· ⟨V⟩

atsu·i

atataka·i

suzushi·i

samu·i

kaze ⟨N⟩
kaze ga fuk· ⟨V⟩

yuki ⟨N⟩
yuki ga fur· ⟨V⟩

Tenki-yohō ⟨Weather Forecast⟩

Hare, nochi kumori.
   ⟨Fine, later cloudy.⟩

Kumori, tokidoki ame.
   ⟨Cloudy, with occasional rain.⟩

Kumori, ichiji yuki.
   ⟨Cloudy, with brief snows.⟩

Haretari, kumottari.
   ⟨Alternately clear and cloudy.⟩

taifū ⟨typhoon⟩

tsuyu ⟨rainy season—June⟩

New Words For UNIT 15

asa·i	shallow
atsu·i	thick, bulky
	Cf. atsu·i hot
...de(wa)	→KS
dore	which one? →FS & U-4 FS
fuka·i	deep
futo·i	thick, big →LL
Gōruden-batto	←Golden Bat ⟨brand of Japanese cigarettes⟩
hiku·i	low
hō	⟨N⟩ direction →KS
hoso·i	thin, slender, narrow →LL
ichiban	most →KS
jin	←gin
keisan-ki	calculator
	keisan ⟨Nv⟩ calculation
kō-cha	black tea
	Cf. o-cha green tea; tea
konna	this kind of →FS
mijika·i	short
mikan	orange, tangerine
sema·i	narrow, small, not spacious
	Cf. hiro·i wide, spacious
soroban	Japanese abacus →U-19 LL
tokai	(big) city
	Cf. shuto capital city; dai-tokai big city; machi town; inaka countryside; nō-son agricultural village; gyo-son fishing village
tsuyo·i	strong
uchi	inside (=naka); house; my house/company/school etc.
uokka	⟨←Russian *vodka*⟩
usu·i	thin, faint
waka·i	young
	Cf. wakamono youth,

young man
| ...yori | than/from... →KS |
| zutto | much (more) →KS |

♦ Some Popular Japanese Names

Family	Male	Female
Satō	Hiroshi	Yoshiko
Suzuki	Toshio	Keiko
Takahashi	Yoshio	Kazuko
Itō	Kazuo	Hiroko
Watanabe	Akira	Yōko
Saitō	Masao	Masako
Tanaka	Takashi	Toshiko
Kobayashi	Hideo	Michiko
Sasaki	Kiyoshi	Sachiko
Yamamoto	Minoru	Fumiko

(Courtesy of Nippon Univac Kaisha, Ltd.)

UNIT 15
To Make COMPARISONS

● Key Structures

1. Ringo to mikan dewa, dochira no hō ga ōki·i desu ka?
   —Ringo no hō ga ōki·i desu.
2. Ringo wa mikan yori ōki·i desu.
3. Kudamono no naka dewa, nani ga ichiban oishi·i desu ka?

---

1 N_1 **to** N_2 **dewa, dochira (no hō) ga** $N(a)/A·i$ **desu ka?**

Which is more Na/A, N_1 or N_2?

$(N_1$ **yori)** N_2 **no hō ga** $N(a)/A·i$ **desu.**

N_2 is more Na/A (than N_1).

Japanese has no distinctive comparative or superlative forms.

2 N_1 **wa** N_2 **yori** $N(a)/A·i$ **desu.** N_1 is more Na/A than N_2.

The Postposition yori functions like the English 'than.' When you want to emphasize the comparison, put zutto before the Na/A/Adv.

3 $\left.\begin{array}{l} N_1 \text{ **to** } N_2 \text{ **to** } N_3 \\ \text{[Group/Place]} \end{array}\right\}$ **(no** $\left\{\begin{array}{l} \textbf{naka} \\ \textbf{uchi} \end{array}\right\}$**) de(wa),** N **ga ichiban** $\left\{\begin{array}{l} N(a) \\ A·i \end{array}\right\}$ **desu.**

N is the most Na/A, among N_1, N_2, and N_3/of [Group]/in [Place].

When you want to express the superlative, put ichiban before Na/A/Adv. The Postpositional phrase ...(no naka/uchi) de(wa) functions just like the English 'among/of/in.' The Interrogatives are nani ⟨what⟩, dore ⟨which one⟩, dare ⟨who⟩, or doko ⟨where⟩.

1. Which is bigger, an apple or an orange?

   —An apple is bigger.

2. An apple is bigger than an orange.

3. What fruit tastes best?

★More Examples For Practice

1 Kore **to** are **dewa**, **dochira** (**no hō**) **ga** yasu·i desu **ka?**

   —Kore **no hō ga** yasu·i desu.

   Keisan-ki **to** soroban **dewa**, **dochira** (**no hō**) ga benri desu **ka?**

   —Keisan-ki (**no hō ga** benri) desu.

2 Kono nekutai wa ano nekutai **yori** zutto taka·i desu.

   Chika-tetsu wa basu **yori** benri desu.= Basu **yori** chika-tetsu no hō ga benri desu.=Chika-tetsu no hō ga basu **yori** benri desu.

3 Satō-san **to** Suzuki-san **to** Itō-san (**no naka**) **dewa**, dare ga **ichiban** waka·i desu ka?

   —Itō-san (ga **ichiban** waka·i) desu.

   Nippon no kamera (**no naka**) **de**, dore ga **ichiban** i·i desu ka?

   Amerika no tokai (**no naka**) **de**, doko ga **ichiban** ōki·i desu ka?

1 Which is cheaper, this one or that one?

—This one is cheaper.

Which is more convenient, an electric calculator or a soroban?

—An electric calculator is.

2 This necktie is much more expensive than that necktie.

Subways are more convenient than buses.

3 Among Sato, Suzuki, and Ito, who is the youngest?

—Ito is.

What is the best Japanese camera?

What is the biggest city in the USA?

● Further Study

ko~ ; so~ ; a~ ; do~   →Unit 1 ⑤, Unit 2 ③, & Unit 3 ④

	This one	This N	This place	This direction	Like this	Thus
Near the speaker	kore	kono N	koko	kochira	konna	kō
Near the listener	sore	sono N	soko	sochira	sonna	sō
Away from both	are	ano N	asoko	achira	anna	ā
Interrogative	dore	dono N	doko	dochira	donna	dō

Japanese has three Demonstratives ko~, so~, and a~ and one Interrogative do~, which are declined as shown in the above table.

As you have learned, ko~ is used to indicate something near the speaker, so~ near the listener, and a~ away from both. Yet this distance is not only spatial but also psychological and temporal distance. So when you are talking about a person/thing/topic which you have mentioned yourself, you can use ko~ as the Demonstrative like the English 'it,' and when it is a person/thing/topic the listener has mentioned, you can use so~. By the same token, when it is a person/thing/topic that you feel is somewhat "distant," you can use a~.

Dore means 'which one,' not 'what.'

Kochira, sochira, and achira are occasionally used to mean 'this/that one as contrasted with the other.' These can be used to indicate persons. Dochira can be used in place of dore, doko, dare.

Konna, sonna, and anna mean 'such…as this/that' and, when followed by -ni, can be used as Adverbial to express Degree.

Kō, sō, and ā are Adverbs which mean 'in this/that manner.' Dō is used for asking 'how.'

●Conversation

KŌHĪ, KŌ-CHA.... DOCHIRA?———《At The Party》

Kōhī? Kōcha?... Dochira?

—Kōhī.

*　*　*

Wain to uisukī dewa, dochira no hō ga i·i desu ka?

—Wain no hō ga i·i desu.

*　*　*

Jin wa uisukī yori tsuyo·i desu.

*　*　*

Jin to uisukī to uokka no naka de, dore ga ichiban tsuyo·i desu ka?

—Sā?... Uokka ga ichiban tsuyo·i yō desu.

*　*　*

—Nippon no tabako no naka de, nani ga ichiban yasu·i desu ka?

Gōruden-batto desu.

*　*　*

Amerika no uisukī to Igirisu no uisukī dewa, dochira no hō ga oishi·i desu ka???

Coffee? Tea? Which?
—Coffee.

*　*　*

Which do you prefer, wine or whiskey?
—I prefer wine.

*　*　*

Gin is stronger than whiskey.

*　*　*

Which is strongest, gin, whiskey, or vodka?
—Well, let's see…. It seems vodka is strongest.

*　*　*

—What is the cheapest Japanese tobacco?
'Golden Bat' is.

*　*　*

Which is better tasting, American whiskey or British whiskey???

▼Japanese tobacco

●Look & Learn

Adjectives Compared

ōki·i   chiisa·i

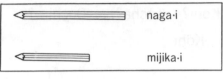

naga·i

mijika·i

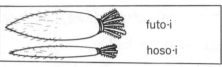

futo·i

hoso·i

omo·i   karu·i

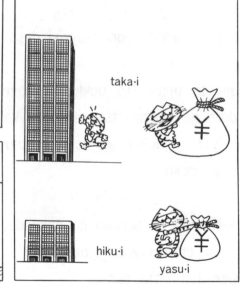

taka·i

hiku·i

yasu·i

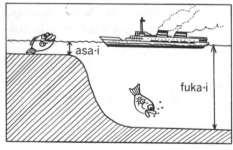

asa·i

fuka·i

hiro·i   sema·i

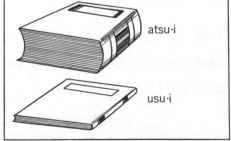

atsu·i

usu·i

New Words For UNIT 16

ak·	to open ⟨Vi⟩
	Cf. ake· to open ⟨Vt⟩
ane	older sister →U-7 LL
ani	older brother →U-7 LL
atsume·	to collect, gather ⟨Vt⟩
bessō	villa
dō	how? →U-4 FS & U-15 FS
	Dō shite imasu ka? ⟨Cph⟩
	How is [Person]?
go-	⟨Honorific for Noun⟩
go-kekkon	(your) marriage
hisashiburi	⟨N⟩ after a long time
	Hisashiburi desu ne. ⟨Cph⟩
	I haven't seen you for a
	long time.
hitori-de	alone, by oneself
	hitori one person→U-6 FS
hon-sha	head/main office
	Cf. shi-sha branch office
i·	to exist, be, stay
	V·te i· be doing... →KS
	...ga i· There be... ⟨Ani-
	mate⟩ →U-3
Kamakura	⟨place name⟩ →U-17 LL
kangae·	to think, consider
kitte	postage stamp
kusuri	medicine
	kusuri o nom· to take
	medicine
Kyashī	←Cathy
mada	yet, still
...mae	⟨N/Adv⟩ [Period of time]
	ago/before →U-29 FS
minna	⟨N/Adv⟩ everybody,
	everything
mot·	to hold, grasp, have
	motte i· to have, possess
	→KS & FS
nak·	to weep, cry; chirp; whine

nemur·	to sleep
...niwa	...ni+wa →U-19 KS &
	FS
nyūin	⟨Nv⟩ being hospitalized
obā-san	grandmother →U-7 LL
oji	uncle →U-7 LL
Okage-sama-de,	⟨Cph⟩ Thanks to
	you, ⟨This phrase is often
	used as mere politeness.⟩
otōto-san	younger brother→U-7 LL
ryō	dormitory
ryokō	⟨Nv⟩ travel, trip
sagas·	to search
shaber·	to talk, chat; tell on
shimaw·	to finish; put away
	V·te shimaw· to finish
	doing... →KS
shinbun	newspaper
shinbun-sha	newspaper office
shinpai	⟨Nv/N(a)⟩ worry, anxiety
shir·	to know, become aware of
shizum·	to sink
-shōji	...Commercial Firm
shōsha	trading company
-shū-kan	⟨N/Adv⟩ ...weeks
sofā	←sofa
sum·	to dwell, inhabit
	sunde i· to live, reside
	→KS & FS
sutōbu	←stove
Tokoro-de,	By the way,
Tōzai-shōji	Tozai Trading Company
tsukare·	to get tired
tsutome·	to serve, get employed,
	work at
ur·	to sell
yob·	to call, invite

UNIT 16
To Indicate CONTINUITY

● Key Structures

1. Biru wa soto de asonde imasu.
2. Watashi wa Tōkyō ni sunde imasu.
3. Anata wa Nippon-go no hon o motte imasu ka?
4. Anata wa Yoshida-san o shitte imasu ka?
5. Watashi wa tegami o kaite shimaimashita.

―――

1 | **V·te i·** | be ~ing

You would never say, "I am having a car," in English, but you would say, "I have a car." Why? Because 'have' in this case expresses a situation/state rather than an action. In this way, English verbs can be classified as either ① state verbs or ② action verbs.

Japanese Verbs are typically action verbs; in other words, verbs which express either action or change of state. Therefore, if you want to express a state or continuous action, you must turn to the V·te i· form which is equivalent to the English 'be ~ing' form. For example, mot· means no more than 'to come to hold/possess,' and so, when you want to say 'to have/own,' you have to use motte i·. By the same token, habit may be defined as repetition of the same action, so that hataraite i· (not hatarak·) is used to mean 'to work (in a company)/ have a job.' The result of some action is also regarded as a state and expressed with the V·te i· form. i.e. 'to know' is shitte i· not shir· which means no more than 'to know' in the sense of 'to learn.'

2 | **V·te shimaw·** | complete/finish ~ing

1. Bill is playing outdoors.

2. I live in Tokyo.

3. Do you have a Japanese book?

4. Do you know Mr. Yoshida?

5. I have finished writing a letter.

★More Examples For Practice

① Chichi wa shinbun o yon**de imasu**.

Haha wa tegami o kai**te imasu**.

Imōto wa terebi o mi**te imasu**.

Ani wa rekōdo o kii**te imasu**.

Ima watashi wa Nippon-go o benkyō-**shite imasu**.

Chichi wa shinbun-sha de hatarai**te imasu**.

Oji wa Yokohama ni sun**de imasu**.

Watashi-tachi wa Kamakura ni bessō o mot**te imasu**.

Ane wa daigaku ni it**te imasu**.

Inu wa sutōbu no mae ni suwat**te imasu**.

Neko wa sofā ni ne**te imasu**.

Obā-san wa nyūin-**shite imasu**.

② Watashi wa Nichi-yō(bi) made ni kono hon o yon**de shimaimasu**.

Anata wa mō yon**de shimaimashita** ka?

① Father is reading the newspaper.
Mother is writing a letter.
My younger sister is watching TV.
My older brother is listening to a record.
I'm studying Japanese now.
Father works for a newspaper company.
My uncle lives in Yokohama.
We have a villa in Kamakura.
① My (older) sister goes to college. ② My sister has gone to college.
Our dog is sitting in front of the stove.
Our cat is lying on the sofa.
Grandma is in the hospital.
② I'll finish reading this book by Sunday.
Have you finished reading this?

● Further Study

V•te imasu vs. V•masu

As explained in Unit 16 $\boxed{1}$, V•te i• has three meanings; ① action/event in progress, ② habit, and ③ result or state/condition resulting from a previous action/event. Compare the following examples.

I. Action/Event in Progress

Watashi wa Ōta-san o sagashite imasu. 〈I'm looking for Mr. Ota.〉

Cf. Watashi wa Ōta-san o sagashimasu. 〈I'll look for Mr. Ota.〉

Jon-san wa anata o yonde imashita. 〈John was calling you.〉

Ima watashi wa terebi o mite imasu. 〈I'm watching TV.〉

Keiko-san wa Hokkaidō o ryokō-shite imasu.

〈Keiko is traveling in Hokkaido.〉

II. Habit

Watashi wa kitte o atsumete imasu. 〈I collect stamps.〉

Cf. Watashi wa kitte o atsumemasu. 〈I'll collect stamps.〉

Mai-nichi terebi de Furansu-go o benkyō-shite imasu.

〈I study French on television every day.〉

Jon-san wa kono kusuri o nonde imasu. 〈John takes this medicine.〉

Kono mise wa kamera o utte imasu. 〈This shop sells cameras.〉

III. Result

Chichi wa kaette imasu. 〈Father has come home.〉

Cf. Chichi wa roku-ji ni kaerimasu. 〈Father will come home at six.〉

Ginkō wa mada aite imasu. 〈The bank is still open.〉

Sono fune wa koko ni shizunde imasu. 〈The ship has sunk here.〉

Watashi wa Jon-san o shitte imasu. 〈I know John.〉

NB: The Negative of shitte imasu is not shitte imasen but shiri-masen.

●Conversation

O-GENKI DESU KA?————《How Is Everybody?》

—Yoshida-san, hisashiburi desu ne.

Oku-san mo kodomo-san mo, mina-san, o-genki desu ka?

Okage-sama-de, minna genki desu.

—Otōto-san wa dō shite imasu ka?

Kyonen daigaku o demashita.

Ima shōsha ni tsutomete imasu.

—Doko no shōsha desu ka?

Tōzai-shōji no Tōkyō hon-sha desu.

—Go-kekkon wa?

Mada desu. Hitori-de kaisha no ryō ni sunde imasu.

Tokoro-de Sumisu-san, itsu kochira e kimashita?

—Ni-shū-kan mae desu.

Jā, mō imōto-san niwa aimashita ne?

—Kyashī desu ka? Iya, mada atte imasen. Ima Hokkaidō o ryokō-shite imasu.

Asatte Tōkyō ni kaeru yō desu.

Sō desu ka?...

—Yoshida. Haven't seen you for a long time.
How are your wife and children?

They are fine, thank you.

—How is your brother?

He graduated from college last year. He is working for a trading company now.

—Which one?

Tozai Trading, in the Tokyo office.

—Is he married?

Not yet. He is living alone in the company's dorm.

By the way, Mr. Smith, when did you come here?

—Two weeks ago.

Then you've already met your sister, haven't you?

—You mean Cathy? No, not yet. She's on a trip to Hokkaido.
She's supposed to come back to Tokyo the day after tomorrow.

Oh, really?

▼The Diet Building

●Look & Learn

Kono hito wa nani o shite imasu ka?

⟨What is this person doing?⟩

waratte imasu

naite imasu

kangaete imasu

shinpai-shite imasu

tsukarete imasu

nemutte imasu
nete imasu

hanashite imasu
shabette imasu

koi o shite imasu

New Words For UNIT 17

ar·	to exist, be, stay…
	V·ta-koto ga ar· →KS
ashi	foot; leg
beru	←bell
Bunraku	⟨traditional Japanese puppet theater form⟩
Chūshingura	⟨title of the famous story of the revenge of the 47 samurai⟩
-do	…times (=-kai)
Dōjō-ji	⟨title of a famous play about a lovelorn girl⟩
Ē…to,	⟨Cph⟩ Well; Let me see…,
gorufu	←golf
Honshū	⟨Japan's main island⟩→LL
ichi-do-mo	⟨+Neg.⟩ never, not once
itta-koto	←ik· →KS & U-18 KS & FS
Kabuki	⟨traditional Japanese theater form⟩ →U-19 LL
-ka-getsu	⟨N/Adv⟩ …months →U-29 FS
-kai	…times (=-do) →FS
Kasei	Mars ⟨planet⟩
-koto	→KS & U-18 KS & FS
mannaka	⟨N⟩ right in the middle
metta-ni	⟨+Neg.⟩ seldom, rarely
mita-koto	←mi· →KS & U-18 KS & FS
nan-do-mo	many times
nan-kai-mo	many times
-nen	⟨Suffix for years⟩ e.g. yo-nen four years; rai-nen next year; sen-kyū-hyaku-nana-jū-roku-nen 1976; mai-nen every year
Nihon	Japan (=Nippon)
Nihon-kai	Sea of Japan →LL

Nyū-yōku	←New York
oboe·	to memorize, learn by heart; master
	oboete i· to remember
o-bō-san	(Buddhist) priest, monk
ōkesutora	←orchestra
ōki-na	big ⟨used only as a modifier⟩ Cf. ōki·i
Seto-naikai	Seto Inland Sea →LL
…shika	⟨+Neg.⟩ only, no more than…
Shikashi,	But,
Shikoku	⟨Southern island of Japan⟩ →LL
-shū	⟨Suffix for weeks⟩ e.g. kon-shū this week
-shū-kan	⟨Counter Suffix for weeks⟩ e.g. is-shū-kan (for) one week
Sore-ja,	Then,; Bye. ⟨ja ←dewa⟩
Sō, sō.	⟨Cph⟩ Oh, yes!
sukiyaki	⟨typical Japanese cuisine⟩
sutēji	←stage ⟨of a theater⟩
Taihei-yō	Pacific Ocean →LL Cf. Taisei-yō Atlantic Ocean
tama-ni	occasionally, few and far between
tashika	⟨Adv⟩ if I remember right; perhaps
tōri	street, way
	Sono tōri. ⟨Cph⟩ Exactly.; Right.
Yōroppa	⟨←Portuguese/Dutch *Europa*⟩ Europe
Yū-efu-ō	←UFO ⟨unidentified flying object⟩
zenzen	⟨+Neg.⟩ not at all

UNIT 17
To Refer To Your Own EXPERIENCE

● Key Structures

1. Anata wa Nippon no eiga o mita-koto ga arimasu ka?
   —Hai, mita-koto ga arimasu.

2. Watashi wa ichi-do-mo soko e itta-koto ga arimasen.

3. Ano hito wa metta-ni hon o yomimasen.

4. Watashi wa tama-ni shika terebi o mimasen.

----

1 | **N wa V·ta-koto ga ar·** | N has (once) done....

'N wa' indicates that N is the Topic. Therefore 'N wa' can mean 'The topic is N.' 'As for N,' 'Speaking of N,'. ➡ Unit 19 ③ V·ta-koto literally means 'having done...' so the above Construction may mean, 'For N, having done... exists,' that is, 'N has (once) done....'

NB: ...e/ni itta-koto ga ar· means 'to have been to....'

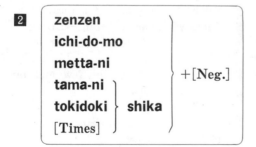

2		
zenzen		not at all
ichi-do-mo		not even once
metta-ni	+[Neg.]	seldom
tama-ni		only a few times
tokidoki ⎬ shika		only sometimes
[Times]		only [Times]

These Adverbials of frequency are always used with Negatives. Tama-ni/tokidoki/[Times] shika +[Neg.] may seem to be negative in meaning, but these are affirmative. Be careful. They are negative only in the sense of 'no more than...,' which is really affirmative. [Times] indicates 'once,' 'twice,' etc. Other Adverbials of frequency are introduced in FS.

1. Have you ever seen a Japanese movie?

    —Yes, I have.

2. I have never been there.

3. He seldom reads books.

4. I seldom watch television.

★More Examples For Practice

1 (Anata wa) Yōroppa e it**ta-koto ga arimasu** ka?

    —Hai, nan-do-mo (it**ta-koto ga**) **arimasu**.

    Ashi o ot**ta-koto ga arimasu** ka?

    —Iie, ichi-do-mo **arimasen**.

    Sukiyaki o tabe**ta-koto ga arimasu** ka?

    —Hai, yoku tabemasu.

    Watashi wa nan-kai-mo 'Yū-efu-ō' o mi**ta-koto ga arimasu**. Kasei-jin ni at**ta-koto mo arimasu**.

2 Watashi wa **zenzen** gorufu o shita-koto ga ari**masen**. Anata wa arimasu ka?

    —Hai, nan-do-mo arimasu.

    Watashi wa **tama-ni shika** tabako o sui**masen**.

    Watashi wa Tanaka-san ni ni-**kai shika** atta-koto ga ari**masen**.

    Chichi wa **metta-ni** rajio o kiki**masen**.

    Imōto wa itsu-mo sutereo o kiite imasu.

1 Have you ever been to Europe?

—Yes, many times.

Have you ever broken a leg?

—No, never.

Have you ever eaten suki-yaki?

—Yes, often.

I've seen several UFO's and have even talked with a Martian.

2 I've never played golf. Have you?

—Yes, many times.

I smoke only occasionally.

I've seen Tanaka only twice.

Father seldom listens to the radio.

My younger sister is always listening to her stereo set.

● Further Study

How to Make V•**ta** Forms

$$V \cdot \underline{te} \longrightarrow V \cdot \underline{ta}$$

Cf. V•te → Unit 12 FS

e.g. mi• → mi**ta**

tabe• → tabe**ta**

kik• → ki**ita**

ik• → i**tta**

yom• → yo**nda**

Adverbials of Frequency

I.
tama-ni	from time to time
tokidoki	sometimes
nan-kai-mo/nan-do-mo	many times
yoku	often
itsu-mo/itsu-demo	always/anytime

II. mai- ⟨every...⟩

mai-nichi	every day	mai-asa	every morning
mai-ban	every evening	mai-shū	every week
mai-tsuki	every month	mai-nen	every year

III. -kai ⟨...times a day/year etc.⟩ Cf. Unit 29 FS

ichi-nichi ni ik-kai	once a day
is-shū-kan ni ni-kai	twice a week
ik-ka-getsu ni san-kai	three times a month
ichi-nen ni yon-kai	four times a year

NB: The counting of times sounds the same as that of floors, except
for san-kai ⟨three times⟩ ⟨Cf. the third floor: san-gai⟩, but their
pitches ⟨→p. 7⟩ are different.

●Conversation

SŌ, SONO TŌRI.————《Have You Seen Kabuki?》

Kabuki o mita-koto ga arimasu ka?

—Hai, arimasu.

Bunraku wa?

—Bunraku mo mimashita. Shikashi,
   Kabuki no hō ga omoshiro·i desu.

Nani o mimashita?

—Ē...to, namae wa oboete imasen.

Doko de mimashita ka?

—San-nen mae ni Nyū-yōku de
   mimashita.

Sore-ja, ... tashika 'Chūshingura'
deshita ne.

—Sō kamo shiremasen. Sutēji no
   ushiro no ōkesutora ga taihen
   kirei deshita. Sutēji no mannaka
   ni ōki-na beru ga arimashita.

Ā, sore wa 'Dōjō-ji' no hazu desu.

Takusan o-bō-san ga ita deshō?

—Sō, sō, sono tōri desu.

Watashi wa Bunraku no 'Dōjō-ji' mo
mita-koto ga arimasu.

Have you ever seen kabuki?
—Yes, I have.
How about bunraku?
—Yes, I saw bunraku, too.
   But I found kabuki more
   interesting.
What did you see?
—Well, I don't remember
   the title of the play.
Where did you see it?
—In New York three years
   ago.
Then, perhaps it was *Chu-shingura*.
—Maybe so. The orchestra
   on back stage was very
   beautiful. In the center
   of the stage was a big bell.
Oh, that must be *Dojo-ji*.
There were many monks on
stage, weren't there?
—Yes, sure, you're right.
I saw *Dojo-ji* as bunraku,
too.

▼Dojo-ji

●Look & Learn

Anata wa _____ e itta koto ga arimasu ka?

⟨Have you ever been to _____?⟩

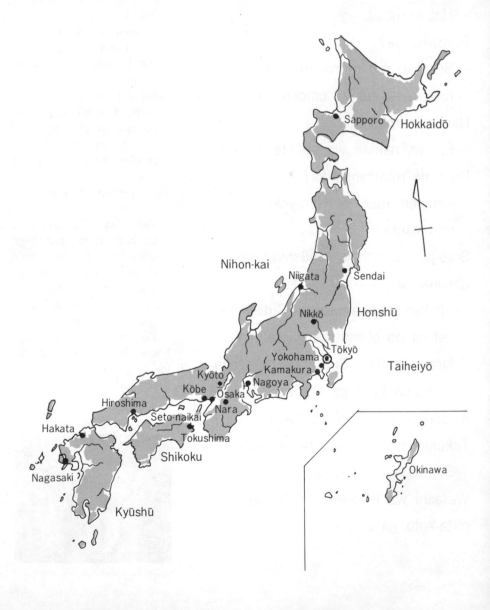

New Words For UNIT 18

ai	⟨Nv⟩ love, affection
amari	⟨+Neg.⟩ not so...
chesu	←chess
chiisa-na	small ⟨used only as a modifier⟩ Cf. chiisa·i
...dake	...alone, only...
de·	to come/go out, appear, show up
	...ni de· to attend, take part in...
	...o/kara de· to come/go out of..., leave...
deki·	to be produced/made/born; be possible →KS
egao	smiling face
futari	two persons →U-6 FS
Hajimemashite.	⟨Cph⟩ How do you do?
hanasu-koto	←hanas· →KS
hanasu-no	←hanas· →KS
heta-na	unskillful, clumsy →KS
hik·	to pull
	gitā/piano o hik· to play the guitar/piano
hitomi	pupil of the eye
Hora,	Look,; Listen,
hoshi·i	desirable →U-20 KS
ichi-do	once
inochi	life
inor·	to pray
jibun-de	for/by oneself
jōzu-na	skillful →KS
kādo	←card, playing cards
kanari	quite
mama	←mama
māmā	moderate, so-so
Mā ne.	⟨Cph⟩ Well, you know.
muzukashi·i	difficult
nakigoe	⟨N⟩ cry; whine

	Cf. nak· to cry; whine
naraw·	to learn, practice
	...kara/ni naraw· to learn from...
negai	⟨N⟩ wish, desire, prayer
-niku·i	hard to do... →FS
...no.	→U-27 FS
-no	→KS & FS
nozomi	⟨N⟩ hope, wish, prospect
o-negai	⟨Nv⟩ appeal, wish
	O-negai(-shimasu). ⟨Cph⟩ Please, (do...for me).
papa	←papa
piano	←piano
ryōri	⟨Nv⟩ cooking
shiawase	⟨N/N(a)⟩ happiness
shirushi	sign, mark, symbol
sodat·	to grow ⟨Vi⟩
	sodate to inor· to pray for one's growth
sore-hodo	to that extent
	Sore-hodo demo arimasen. ⟨Cph⟩ Not really.; Not all that much.
sukī	←ski, skiing
sukoyaka-na	healthy
te	hand; arm
tokidoki-wa	from time to time, sometimes (at least)
Tomu	←Tom
tsubura-na	round/beady ⟨of eyes⟩
tsukur·	to make, produce
	tsukutte hoshi·i I want you to make...
unten	⟨Nv⟩ driving
uta	song
	Cf. utaw· to sing
utsukushi·i	beautiful
-yasu·i	easy to do... →FS

UNIT 18
To Express ABILITY

● Key Structures

1. Watashi wa Ei-go o hanasu-koto ga dekimasen.
2. Anata wa tenisu ga dekimasu ka?
   —Hai, dekimasu.
3. Tanaka-san wa Supein-go o hanasu-no ga jōzu desu.
4. Watashi wa gorufu ga heta desu.

---

1 | N wa V·u-koto ga deki· | N can do. . . .

This Construction literally means, 'With N, doing . . . is possible,' which easily translates as 'N can do. . . .'

2 | N wa [Something] ga deki· | N can do [Something].

If Construction ① has [Something]-suru-koto or [Something] o suru-koto, then the -suru-koto or o suru-koto can be omitted to make Construction ②. Some other V·u-koto can be omitted as well.

3 | N wa V·u-no ga jōzu/heta desu. | N is good/poor at doing. . . .

Jōzu, heta are N(a).

4 | N wa [Something] ga jōzu/heta desu. |

N is good/poor at doing [Something].

Look at the transformation principles in ② and ⑤.

5 | Vᴾ-koto ≒ Vᴾ-no |

These are Nominalization of Verbs or Clauses. ➡FS
The difference in usage will be shown in Unit 26 FS.

1. I cannot speak English.
2. Can you play tennis?

   —Yes, I can.
3. Mr. Tanaka is good at speaking Spanish.
4. I am bad at golf.

★More Examples For Practice

1 Watashi **wa** ōtobai o unten-**suru-koto ga dekimasu**.

Anata **wa** piano o hik**u-koto ga dekimasu** ka?

—Iie, **dekimasen**.

Watashi **wa** Roshia-go o hanas**u-koto ga dekimasen**.

2 Watashi **wa** ōtobai no unten **ga dekimasu**.

Anata **wa** Ei-go **ga dekimasu** ka?

—Hai, sukoshi **dekimasu**.

—Iie, amari **dekimasen**.

3 Ane **wa** uta o uta**u-no ga jōzu desu**.

Watashi **wa** ryōri o tsukur**u-no ga heta desu**.

4 Ane **wa** uta **ga jōzu desu**.

Watashi **wa** ryōri **ga heta desu**.

Tomu-san **wa** chesu ya kādo **ga** taihen **jōzu desu**. Watashi **wa** amari **jōzu dewa arimasen**.

Watashi **wa** Nippon-go **ga heta desu**.

---

1 I can ride a motorcycle.
Can you play the piano?
—No, I can't.
I cannot speak Russian.

2 I can ride a motorcycle.
Can you speak English?
—Yes, a little.
—No, not so well.

3 My older sister sings well.
I am a bad cook.

4 My older sister sings well.
I am a bad cook.
Tom is very good at chess and cards. I am not very good.
My Japanese is terrible.

● Further Study

Some Words Derived From Verbs

I. Verbal Nouns

  (1) V^P-koto ⟨what one does/did⟩

      e.g. hanas· ⟨to speak⟩→ hanasu-koto ⟨what one speaks⟩

                          hanashita-koto ⟨what one spoke⟩

      NB: V^P-koto as well as V^P-no ⟨➡Unit 26 FS⟩ has the other func-
      tion of making a Noun clause for the sentence, in which case 'N
      wa' is replaced by 'N ga/o' ⟨➡Unit 19 ③⟩.

      e.g. Watashi wa kare ni aimashita. ⟨I met him.⟩

          →Watashi ga kare ni atta-koto

            ⟨(the fact) that I met him⟩

  (2) V^v-kata/V^c-i-kata/ki-kata/shi-kata ⟨how to do⟩

      e.g. tabe· ⟨to eat⟩ → tabe-kata ⟨how to eat⟩

          yom· ⟨to read⟩ → yomi-kata ⟨how to read⟩

          kuru ⟨to come⟩→ ki-kata ⟨how to come⟩

          suru ⟨to do⟩ → shi-kata ⟨how to do⟩

  (3) V^c·i/V^v

      e.g. kaer· ⟨to return⟩ → kaeri ⟨way back⟩

          tōr· ⟨to pass by⟩→ tōri ⟨street⟩

II. Verbal Adjectives

  (1) V^v-yasu·i/ V^c·i-yasu·i/ki-yasu·i/shi-yasu·i ⟨easy to do⟩

      e.g. tabe· ⟨to eat⟩ → tabe-yasu·i ⟨easy to eat⟩

          yom· ⟨to read⟩→ yomi-yasu·i ⟨easy to read⟩

  (2) V^v-niku·i/V^c·i-niku·i/ki-niku·i/shi-niku·i ⟨hard to do⟩

      e.g. tabe· ⟨to eat⟩ → tabe-niku·i ⟨hard to eat⟩

          yom· ⟨to read⟩→ yomi-niku·i ⟨hard to read⟩

●Conversation

MĀMĀ DESU.————《Are You A Good Skier?》

Anata wa sukī o shita-koto ga
arimasu ka?

—Ē, demo, ichi-do shika shita-koto ga
  arimasen. Taihen heta desu.
  Sukī wa muzukashi·i desu ne.

Magaru-koto ga dekimasu ka?

—Iie, dekimasen. Tomaru-no mo
  muzukashi·i desu.
  Anata wa jōzu desu ka?

Māmā desu.

—Sore-ja, tomaru-koto mo dekimasu
  ne.

Mā ne.

—Dare ni naraimashita ka?

Naratta-koto wa arimasen.

—Ichi-do-mo?

Hai, jibun-de oboemashita.

Mukashi Hokkaidō ni sunde imashita.

—Sō desu ka? Dewa, kanari jōzu
  deshō ne. . . .

Iya, sore-hodo demo arimasen.

Have you ever gone skiing?
—Yes, but only once. I'm
a very bad skier. Skiing
is very difficult.
Can you turn?
—No, I can't. It's also hard
for me to stop.
Are you good at it?
So-so.
—Then, you can stop, can't
you?
Sort of.
—Who taught you?
I've never had lessons.
—Not even once?
No, I learned by myself.
I used to live in Hokkaido.
—Oh, you did? Then, you
must be quite good, I
suppose.
No, not really.

●Look & Learn

Nippon no uta o utaimashō! 〈Let's Sing!〉

KONNICHIWA, AKA-CHAN!

❶ Konnichiwa, aka-chan!
Anata no egao.
Konnichiwa, aka-chan!
Anata no nakigoe,
Sono chiisa-na te,
Tsubura-na hitomi.
Hajimemashite!
Watashi ga Mama yo.

❷ Konnichiwa, aka-chan!
Anata no inochi.
Konnichiwa, aka-chan!
Anata no mirai ni,
Kono shiawase ga
Papa no nozomi yo.
Hajimemashite!
Watashi ga Mama yo.

❸ Futari dake no
Ai no shirushi,
Sukoyaka-ni, utsukushi·ku
Sodate to inoru.
Konnichiwa, aka-chan!
O-negai ga aru no;
Konnichiwa, aka-chan!
Tokidoki-wa Papa to,

❹ Hora, futari dake no
Shizuka-na yoru o
Tsukutte hoshi·i no.
Oyasumi-nasai.

O-negai, aka-chan!
Oyasumi, aka-chan!
Watashi ga Mama yo.

Lyrics by Rokusuke Ei
Music by Hachidai Nakamura

ⓒ1963 R. Ei, H. Nakamura, Watanabe Music Pub. Corp.
Used by permission of JASRAC Licence No.8324006-831

New Words For UNIT 19

-ban ⟨Counter Suffix⟩ No.
E? ⟨Cph⟩ What?; Beg your pardon?
ekonomī-kurasu ←economy class
fāsuto-kurasu ←first class
gaikoku foreign country
Cf. gaikoku-jin/gai-jin forcigncr
gaikoku-ryokō ⟨Nv⟩ overseas travel
geta ⟨Japanese wooden clogs⟩
Gurīn-sha ←Green Cars ⟨nickname for lst class cars on Japanese National Railways⟩
hajimete ⟨N/Adv⟩ for the first time
Hawai ←Hawaii
-kai-me ⟨Counter Suffix⟩ ⟨N⟩ the ~th time
kimono ⟨Japanese clothing⟩

madoguchi wicket, window
midori ⟨N⟩ green
Midori no Madoguchi Green Window ⟨Japanese National Railways reservation window for long-distance express tickets⟩
Nihon-ryōri Japanese cuisine
Nō ⟨traditional Japanese masked play⟩
pachinko ⟨Nv⟩ ⟨very popular Japanese pinball game⟩
tenpura ⟨typical Japanese cuisine⟩

+++++++++++++++++++++++++++

Hello, little baby! ⟨Translation of the song on page 118⟩

① Hello, little baby!
Your smiling face.
Hello, little baby!
Your cry,
Your tiny hands,
Your bright, little eyes.
How do you do?
I am your mother.

② Hello, little baby!
This life of yours.
Hello, little baby!
In all your days
May you have this happiness.
That is your father's wish.
How do you do?
I am your mother.

③ This symbol of our love,
May you healthily and beautifully
Grow up, we pray.
Hello, little baby!
I have a request of you;
Hello, little baby!
Will you sometimes,

④ For just your daddy and me,
Give us a quiet evening?
I pray of you, baby,
Please go to sleep.

Please, little baby!
Go to sleep, little baby!
I am your mother.

UNIT 19
To Say This Is The FIRST TIME

● Key Structures

1. Watashi wa o-tera o miru-no ga hajimete desu.
2. Anata wa sukī ga hajimete desu ka?

   —Iie, hajimete dewa arimasen.

   Nan-kai-mo shita-koto ga arimasu.

---

1 | **N wa V·u-no ga hajimete desu.** | N does ... for the first time.

Hajimete is a Noun meaning 'the first time,' so this Construction literally means, 'With N, doing ... is the first time,' which easily translates as 'This is the first time for N to do....'

2 | **N wa [Something] ga hajimete desu.**

N does [Something] for the first time.

Look at the transformation principles in Unit 18 **2** and **5**.

3 | **wa** vs. **ga**

In Japanese, generally speaking, Agents are followed by ga, while Topics are indicated by wa ⟨→Unit 17 **1**⟩. Therefore, you'll sometimes see both wa and ga in the same sentence. When the Agent happens to be the Topic, it takes wa. The Topic is not necessarily an Agent; it can be any word or phrase to which the speaker wants to direct the listener's attention.

Interrogatives like nani, dare, doko, etc. never take wa, because something which is unknown to the speaker cannot be the Topic.

'N o V' can be 'N wa V' when N is chosen as the Topic. →FS

1. This is the first time I've ever seen a temple.

2. Is this your first time to ski?

   —No, this isn't my first time.

   I've skied several times.

★More Examples For Practice

1. Watashi **wa** Nippon e iku**-no ga haji-mete desu**.

   (Anata **wa**) gaikoku o ryokō-**suru-no ga hajimete desu** ka?

   —Iie, **hajimete dewa arimasen**.

   Yamada-san ni au**-no wa hajimete desu**.

   Nippon-jin to Nippon-go de hanasu**-no wa hajimete** desu ka?

   —Iie, Hawai de nan-do-mo (hanashita-koto ga) arimasu.

2. Watashi **wa** gaikoku-ryokō **ga hajimete desu**.

   Anata **wa** Nippon **ga hajimete desu** ka?

   —Iie, Ōsaka e kita-koto ga arimasu.

   Shikashi, Kyōto **wa hajimete desu**.

   Nihon-ryōri **wa hajimete dewa arima-sen**.

   Sushi ya tenpura ya sukiyaki o tabeta-koto ga arimasu.

1. This is the first time for me to go to Japan.

   Is this the first time for you to travel abroad?

   —No, it's not my first time.

   This is the first time I've met Mr. Yamada.

   Is this the first time for you to speak Japanese with a Japanese?

   —No, I've spoken it several times in Hawaii.

2. This is my first trip abroad.

   Is this your first visit to Japan?

   —No, I've been to Osaka.

   But I've never been to Kyoto.

   This isn't my first Japanese food.

   I've had sushi, tempura, and sukiyaki before.

● Further Study

wa vs. mo

When you intend to refer to a person/thing/matter, you may be aware of the person/thing/matter as one constituent of a certain group. If you refer to the person/thing/matter contrasting it with other members of the same group, the word(s) indicating it is/are followed by wa. If you refer to it as a representative of the group, the word(s) is/are followed by mo. For example, if you say, "Jon-san wa isha desu." ⟨John is a doctor.⟩, you may have recognized 'John' as one person in a group and have contrasted him with the people 'Andy,' 'Bill,' etc., whereas if you say, "Jon-san mo isha desu." ⟨John is also a doctor.⟩, you may have recognized him as a representative of the group made up of other people 'Eddy,' 'Tom,' etc. who are also doctors. In Japanese, when something is chosen as the Topic, it has necessarily been categorized in a group, although the constituents may, in a strict sense, have no logically common features. Therefore, such Topics are always followed by wa.

On the other hand, ga should be attached to an Agent, which is, as it were, 'given.' For example, if you say, "Koko ni hon ga arimasu," hon is given in the sense that the speaker has not chosen hon as the Topic, but when he intends to refer to what is there, hon happens to be there. And if he didn't mention hon, the listener couldn't understand what is there. Therefore, ga, not wa is attached to Interrogatives, because what the speaker does not know can never be categorized or chosen as the Topic.

Wa or mo can be added even if the Noun has been already followed by another Postposition, unless this Postposition is ga, o, or no. Even if the Postposition is ga or o, wa or mo can replace it. Not so with no. You can not choose N_1 of 'N_1 no N_2' as the Topic.

●Conversation

HAJIMETE DESU.————————《Buying The Ticket》

—Watashi wa Shinkansen ni noru-no
 ga hajimete desu. Doko de kippu
 o kaimasu ka?
Asoko no Midori no Madoguchi desu.

*   *   *

—Koko de Shinkansen no kippu o
 kau-koto ga dekimasu ka?
Hai, dochira made?
—Kyōto made desu.
Gurīn-sha desu ka?
—E? Sore wa nan desu ka?
Fāsuto-kurasu desu.
—Ekonomī-kurasu wa arimasu ka?
Jā, nana-ban ka hachi-ban no
madoguchi e itte kudasai.

*   *   *

—Are wa Fuji-san desu ne.
Sō desu. Anata wa Nippon wa
hajimete desu ka?
—Hai.
Dochira kara?
—Amerika desu.

—This is my first trip on the
  Shinkansen.   Where can
  I buy my ticket?
At the 'Green Window' over
there.

*   *   *

—Can I buy a Shinkansen
  ticket here?
Yes, for where?
—Kyoto.
'Green' Car?
—What? What's that?
First Class.
—Do you have economy class?
Then please go to the No. 7
or No. 8 window.

*   *   *

—That's Mt. Fuji, isn't it?
Right.   Is this your first
visit to Japan?
—Yes.
Where are you from?
—The States.

▼Midori no Madoguchi

●Look & Learn

Things Japanese

kimono

geta

soroban

pachinko

Kabuki

Nō

o-tera

jinja

New Words For UNIT 20

byuffe	←buffet	pinpon	←ping-pong
dansu	⟨Nv⟩ ←dance	riyō	⟨Nv⟩ utilize, make use of
e·	to get, acquire	sake	⟨Japanese alcoholic drink⟩
gitā	←guitar	sanpo	⟨Nv⟩ stroll, walk
Hakata	⟨place name⟩ →U-17 LL		...o sanpo-suru to take a
jetto-ki	←jet plane		walk in...
jūsu	←juice	shokudō-sha	restaurant car
kirai-na	detestable →KS		shokudō restaurant
koibito	lover, sweetheart Cf. koi		(=resutoran)
kom·	to get crowded/full		-sha ...car
	konde i· to be crowded/full	suiei	⟨Nv⟩ swimming
mas·	to increase		Cf. oyog· to swim
mō-sugu	soon, in a moment	sukēto	⟨Nv⟩ ←skating
nobi·	to extend, stretch ⟨Vi⟩	suki-na	fond, like →KS
o-sake	=sake		

╋╋╋╋╋╋╋╋╋╋╋╋╋╋╋╋╋╋╋╋╋╋

Is an Adjective ending in ~i N(a) or A·i?

As you have learned, Na takes the form of N(a) before desu, dewa, etc. and this N(a) often has ~i as its ending. In this case, you may make the mistake of regarding an N(a) ending in ~i as an A·i, for the dot '·' in A·i is not usually written except in this book. Here is a way to distinguish N(a) from A·i.

All A·i have ~ai, ~ii, ~oi, or ~ui as their ending. Therefore, if a given Adjective, before desu, dewa, etc., has any ending other than ~ai, ~ii, ~oi, or ~ui, it is an N(a). However very few N(a) have ~ai, ~ii, ~oi, or ~ui as their ending. (In this respect, you can find only one example of an N(a) ending in ~ai in this book, i.e. kirai.) Consequently, if a given Adjective, except kirai, has C+ Vw, ~n, or ~ei as its ending before desu, dewa, etc., it is an N(a). And if it has ~ai, ~ii, ~oi, or ~ui, it is an A·i.

This rule is applicable to almost all the Adjectives, not only those in this book. That is, if you memorize the few exceptional N(a) ending in ~ai, ~ii, ~oi, or ~ui, you can easily distinguish N(a) from A·i.

NB: Because the ~ei in N(a) is usually pronounced ~ē ⟨→p. 7⟩, this rule can be made even simpler for Colloquial Japanese. That is, if an Adjective has Vw+i, it is an A·i; if not, it is an N(a).

UNIT 20
To Express A PREFERENCE

● Key Structures

1. Watashi wa kōen o sanpo-suru-no ga suki desu.
2. Anata wa sukiyaki ga kirai desu ka?
3. Watashi wa supōtsu-kā ga hoshi·i desu.
4. Watashi wa kōhī no hō ga i·i desu.
5. Anata wa sugu ie e kaetta hō ga i·i desu.

---

1 | **N wa V·u-no ga suki/kirai desu.** | N likes/dislikes doing....

Instead of Verbs meaning 'like, love, dislike, or hate,' the N(a) suki and kirai are usually used. The Negatives and Past forms are made the same as with any Na.

2 | **N wa [Something] ga suki/kirai desu.**

N likes/dislikes [Something].

Look at the transformation principles in Unit 18 **2** and **5**.

3 | **N wa [Something] ga hoshi·i desu.** | N wants to get [Something].

Hoshi·i is an A·i. As for 'want to do...,' ➡Unit 21 **1**.

4 | **N wa [Something] no hō ga i·i desu.** | N prefers [Something].

This is the applied form of Unit 15 **1**.

5 | **N wa Vᴾ hō ga i·i desu.** | N had better do....

This is the applied form of **4**. The Vᴾ usually takes the forms, V·ta/V·nai rather than V·u/V·nakatta.

1. I like walking in the park.

2. Don't you like sukiyaki?

3. I wish I had a sportscar.

4. I prefer coffee.

5. You had better go home at once.

★More Examples For Practice

1. Watashi **wa** oyog**u-no ga suki desu**.

   Biru **wa** eiga o mir**u-no ga suki desu**.

   Anata wa jetto-ki ni nor**u-no ga suki desu** ka?

   —Iie, amari **suki dewa arimasen**.

2. Anata **wa** eiga **ga suki desu** ka?

   —Iie, **kirai desu**.

   Anata **wa** tenpura **ga kirai desu** ka?

   —Iie, **suki desu**.

3. Watashi **wa** jitensha **ga hoshi·i desu**.

   Watashi **wa** koibito **ga hoshi·i desu**.

   Anata **wa** o-kane **ga hoshi·ku-na·i desu** ka?

   —Mochiron, **hoshi·i desu**.

4. Watashi **wa** kō-cha **no hō ga i·i desu**.

   Anata **wa** jūsu **no hō ga i·i desu** ka?

   —Iie, kōhī **no hō ga i·i desu**.

5. Anata **wa** byōin e it**ta hō ga i·i desu**.

   Amari o-sake o noma**nai hō ga i·i desu**.

   Amari tabako o suwa**nai hō ga i·i desu**.

1. I like swimming.
Bill likes watching movies.
Do you like traveling by jet?
  No, I don't like it much.
2. Do you like movies?
—No, I don't.
Don't you like tempura?
—Yes, I do.
3. I want a bicycle.
I wish I had a boyfriend/
girlfriend.
Don't you want any money?
—Yes, of course I do.
4. I prefer tea.
Do you prefer juice?
—No, I prefer coffee.
5. You'd better go to the
hospital.
You'd better not drink too
much.
You'd better not smoke too
much.

●**Further Study**

REVERSE INDEX OF VERB CONJUGATIONS

You have learned so far almost all the conjugated forms of Japanese Verbs. When you are in doubt as to the original or stem form of a given Verb, you can refer to the following list.

NB: (1) This index is applicable not only to the Verbs in this book but to almost all Verbs in contemporary Japanese.

(2) The signs [C] and [Vw], respectively, indicate consonants and vowels other than those given in this index.

~nakereba →~nai	ite ←i·	iyō ←i·
~ida ←~g·	(~)shite ←~s·/suru	shiyō ←suru
~nda ←~b·/m·/n·	~iite ←~ii·/~ik·	~iiyō ←~ii·
~nagara →~masu	kite ←kuru	(~)[C]iyō ←(~)[C]i·
(~)eta ←(~)e·	(~)[C]ite ←(~)[C]i·	koyō ←kuru
ita ←i·	(~)[Vw]ite ←(~)[Vw]k·	~[C]ō ←~[C]·
~mashita →~masu	(~)itte ←ik·/(~)ir·/iw·	(~)[Vw]ō ←(~)[Vw]w·
(~)shita ←~s·/suru	(~)[Vw]tte ←(~)[Vw]r·/	~ru ←~·/~r·
~iita ←~ii·/~ik·	t·/w·	masu ←mas·
kita ←kuru	~nakute →~nai	(~)emasu ←(~)e·
(~)[C]ita ←(~)[C]i·	~anai ←~·	imasu ←i·
(~)[Vw]ita ←(~)[Vw]k·	(~)enai ←(~)e·	~chimasu ←~t·/~chi·
~takunakatta →~masu	inai ←i·	(~)shimasu ←~s·/suru
~nakatta →~nai	shinai ←suru	(~)iimasu ←iw·/~ii·
~takatta →~masu	~iinai ←~ii·	(~)[C]imasu ←~[C]·/
(~)itta ←ik·/(~)ir·/iw·	(~)[C]inai ←(~)[C]i·	(~)[C]i·
(~)[Vw]tta ←(~)[Vw]r·/	konai ←kuru	(~)[Vw]imasu ←(~)[Vw]w·
t·/w·	~takunai →~masu	~tsu ←~t·
~ide ←~g·	~tai →~masu	~[C]u ←~[C]·
~nde ←~b·/m·/n·	~masen →~masu	(~)[Vw]u ←(~)[Vw]w·
(~)ete ←(~)e·	~mashō →~masu	

●Conversation

KONDE IMASU NE.————《In The Super-Express》

—Shinkansen wa benri desu ne.
  Doko kara doko made hashitte
  imasu ka?
Tōkyō kara Hakata made desu.
Mō-sugu Hokkaidō made nobimasu.
—Anata wa yoku Shinkansen o riyō-
  shimasu ka?
Hai. Watashi wa hikō-ki ga amari
suki dewa arimasen.
—Watashi mo kirai desu.

          *   *   *

Issho-ni shokudō-sha e ikimasen ka?
—Ikimashō.

          *   *   *

Konde imasu ne.... Byuffe e itta
hō ga i・i kamo shiremasen.
—Sō shimashō.

          *   *   *

—Watashi wa kōhī ga hoshi・i desu.
  Anata wa?
Watashi wa kō-cha no hō ga i・i
desu.

—The Shinkansen is very
  convenient.
  From where to where does
  this line run?
It runs between Tokyo and
Hakata. Soon it'll be ex-
tended to Hokkaido.
—Do you often use the
  Shinkansen?
Yes. I don't like traveling
by air.
—Neither do I.
          *   *   *
Why don't we go to the
restaurant car together?
—Yes, let's.
          *   *   *
Crowded, isn't it? Perhaps
we'd better go to the buffet
car.
—Let's.
          *   *   *
—I want coffee. You?
I prefer tea.

▼Shinkansen

●Look & Learn

Anata wa _____ ga jōzu/suki/kirai desu ka?
⟨How are you at _____?⟩

tenisu

gorufu

pinpon

suiei

sukī

sukēto

piano

gitā

dansu

uta

e

jidōsha no unten

New Words For UNIT 21

damu	←dam
doko-ka	⟨N⟩ somewhere →U-4 FS
fumikiri	railroad crossing
futari-de	(two persons) together
	Cf. hitori-de by/for one-self, alone
hatake	field, farm
haya·i	fast; early; soon
	Cf. oso·i slow; late
higashi	east
hikō-jō	airport (=kūkō)
	hikō flight
ike	pond
intāchenji	←interchange

itai	want to stay ←i· →KS
itsu-made-mo	forever
jūbun	⟨N(a)/Adv⟩ full, satisfactory
kaeritakunai	don't want to go home ←kaer· →KS
kaigan	beach
kanojo	she
	Cf. kanojo-ra they ⟨female⟩
kazan	volcano
kenbutsu	⟨Nv⟩ sightseeing
kita	north
kōjō	factory

kōsoku-dōro	expressway
Kyōto-kenbutsu	sightseeing in Kyoto
michi	road, way, path, street
minami	south
minato	harbor, port
motto	more, moreover, further
Nara	⟨place name⟩ →U-17 LL
nishi	west
o-ai-suru	=aw· ⟨modest ai: Nominalized form of aw·→U-18 FS I. (3)⟩
O-genki-de.	⟨Cph⟩ Keep well.; Take care of yourself.; See you. →p. 173
oka	hill, rise
omow·	to think →KS
onsen	spa, hot spring
sanbashi	pier, wharf
shima	isle, island
shiyō	←suru →KS
sonna-ni	so (much) →U-15 FS
ta(nbo)	rice field
tekkyō	railroad/iron bridge
tetsudō	railroad
	Cf. chika-tetsu subway; Koku-tetsu Japanese National Railways
...to	that... →KS
tsumori	⟨N⟩ intention, prospect
watas·	to hand over, carry across, transfer, surrender
zehi	by all means, without fail

UNIT 21
To Express Your WISH Or INTENTION

● Key Structures

1. Watashi wa motto Nippon ni itai desu.
2. Amerika ni kaeritakunai desu.
3. Watashi wa Kyōto o kenbutsu-shiyō to omoimasu.
4. Ashita Nara e iku tsumori desu.

---

1 | V·tai desu | want to do...

| V·takunai desu | don't want to do...

You make the V·tai form conjugating the same way as with the V·masu forms, by putting ~tai on V^v and ~itai on V^c. The V·tai forms of V^x are kitai and shitai. ➡FS

V·tai once made conjugates exactly like A·i ⟨➡Unit 10 FS⟩; the Past is V·takatta desu and the Past Negative V·takunakatta desu.

Be careful: 'Want (to get) [Something]' is expressed by '[Something] ga hoshi·i desu.' ➡Unit 20 ③

2 | V·ō to omow· | be planning to do...

For how to make V·ō forms, ➡FS.

3 | V·u/V·nai tsumori desu | intend to/not to do...

Tsumori is a Noun meaning 'intention,' as in the set phrase: Watashi no tsumori dewa, ... ⟨In my intention/As I intend, ...⟩.

1. I want to stay in Japan longer.

2. I don't want to go back to the States.

3. I think I will see the sights of Kyoto.

4. I intend to go to Nara tomorrow.

★More Examples For Practice

1 (Anata wa) haya·ku kuni ni kaeri**tai** desu ka?

—Iie, sonna-ni haya·ku kaeri**takunai** desu. Itsu-made-mo Nippon ni i**tai** desu. Motto Nippon-go o benkyō-**shitai** desu. Nippon o motto shiri**tai** desu.

2 Ashita Nara e ikō **to omoimasu**.

Rai-shū no Getsu-yō(bi) kanojo ni aō **to omoimasu**.

Watashi-tachi wa kekkon-**shiyō to omoimasu**.

Watashi-tachi wa Tōkyō no kōgai ni sumō **to omoimasu**.

3 Rai-shū kare ni au **tsumori** desu.

Watashi wa rikon-**suru tsumori** desu.

Kare niwa kodomo o watasa**nai tsumori** desu.

Kodomo to futari-de Yokohama ni sum**u tsumori** desu.

Ryokō ni ik**u tsumori** desu ka?

—Hai, ikō to omoimasu.

1 Do you want to go home soon?
—No, I don't want to go home so soon. I'd rather stay in Japan forever.
I want to learn Japanese.
I want to know more of Japan.
2 I think I'll go to Nara tomorrow.
I'll meet her next Monday.
We've decided to get married.
We'd like to live in the suburbs of Tokyo.
3 I'm to meet him next week.
I've decided to get a divorce.
I'm not going to let him have our child.
I'll live alone with my child in Yokohama.
Are you going on a trip?
—Yes, I think I will.

● Further Study

How to Make V・**tai** Forms   Cf. V・nai ➡ Unit 10 FS & Unit 13 FS

I. V^v 〈Vowel-ending Verbs〉

V^v + **tai**

e.g.   tabe・ → tabe**tai**
oki・ → oki**tai**

II. V^c 〈Consonant-ending Verbs〉   Cf. Sound Law 〈1〉 ➡ Unit 8 FS

V^c + **i** + **tai**

e.g.   kak・ → kak**itai**
yom・→ yom**itai**
mot・→ mo**chitai**
kaw・→ ka**itai**

III. V^x 〈Irregular Verbs〉

kuru ⟶ **kitai**

suru ⟶ **shitai**

How to Make V・ō Forms

I. V^v 〈Vowel-ending Verbs〉

V^v + **y** + **ō**

e.g.   tabe・→ ・tabe**yō**
oki・ → oki**yō**

II. V^c 〈Consonant-ending Verbs〉

V^c + **ō**

Sound Law 〈3〉

w+ō→ō

e.g.   kak・ → kak**ō**
yom・→ yom**ō**
mot・→ mot**ō**
kaw・→ ka**ō**

III. V^x 〈Irregular Verbs〉

kuru ⟶ **koyō**

suru ⟶ **shiyō**

●Conversation

SĀ, TSUKIMASHITA.————————《A Trip To Kyoto》

—Mō Kyōto desu ka?

Sono yō desu. Anata wa Kyōto de orimasu ka?

—Iai, Kyōto o kenbutsu suru tsumori desu. Furu·i o-tera ya jinja o miyō to omoimasu.

Sō desu ka. Watashi mo Kyōto de orimasu. Mata Kyōto no doko-ka de o-ai-suru kamo shiremasen ne.

—Ē, zehi o-ai-shitai desu ne.

Itsu made Kyōto ni iru o-tsumori desu ka?

—Rai-shū no Getsu-yōbi made iyō to omotte imasu. Ka-yōbi ni Ōsaka e ikanakereba narimasen.

Dewa, jūbun Kyōto-kenbutsu ga dekimasu ne.

* * *

Sā, tsukimashita.

O-genki-de. Sayōnara.

—Sayōnara.

—Are we in Kyoto already?
It seems so. Are you getting off in Kyoto?
—Yes. I intend to do some sightseeing in Kyoto. I think I'll see some old temples and shrines.
Really? I get off here, too. We may meet again somewhere in Kyoto.
—Yes, I hope so.
How long do you plan to stay in Kyoto?
—I'm thinking of staying until next Monday.
I have to go to Osaka on Tuesday.
Then you've got enough time to see Kyoto.

* * *

Here we are.
Have a good time. Bye!
—Good-by!

▼Kiyomizu Temple in Kyoto

●Look & Learn

Let's Read The Map

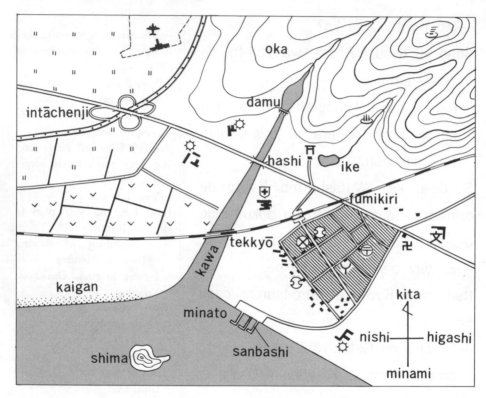

▬▬▬	tetsudō	日 jinja	
▬◆▬	eki	卍 o-tera	
══════	dōro/michi	文 gakkō	
∴∴∴∴	kōsoku-dōro	⊞ byōin	
⚏ kazan		۞ ginkō	
♨ onsen		⊖ yūbin-kyoku	
✈ hikō-jō		⊗ keisatsu(-sho)	
⌄ hatake		Y shōbō-sho	
‖ ta(nbo)		✿ kōjō	

New Words For UNIT 22

ato-de	later, later on
bīfu	←beef
bīru	⟨←Dutch *bier*⟩ beer
-bu	...department/section
bu-chō	director ⟨of a department⟩
chikin	←chicken
denki	electricity; electrical
denwa	⟨Nv⟩ telephone (call)
	denwa ga ar· to get a telephone call
ebi	lobster; prawn; shrimp
ebi-furai	fried prawn
	-furai ←fried...
erekutorikku	←electric
hanbāgā	←hamburger
hikkos·	to move (to a new address)
kani	crab
karē-raisu	←curried rice, curry and rice
Katō	⟨family name⟩
katsu	←cutlet
kime·	to decide
	...ni kime· to decide on... →KS
kon-	this...
	kon-shū this week
kon-getsu	this month
	Cf. rai-getsu next month
	kotoshi this year
nar·	to become; result (in) →p. 83
	...ni nar· →KS
o-denwa	(your) telephone (call) (=denwa)

pōku	←pork
raisu	←rice; boiled rice
	Cf. gohan boiled rice; meal kome rice

raisu   gohan   kome

renraku	⟨Nv⟩ contact; informing
sassoku	immediately, right away
shibaraku	⟨N/Adv⟩ for a while
shutchō	⟨Nv⟩ business trip
sūpu	←soup
suru	do
	...ni suru to decide on... →KS
tamago	egg
tenkin	⟨Nv⟩ being transferred to an office in another city
yoroshi·i	OK, all right
Yū-esu Erekutorikku	←U.S. Electric
yushutsu	⟨Nv⟩ export
	Cf. yunyū ⟨Nv⟩ import
Zannen-nagara,	⟨Cph⟩ To my regret,; I regret to say that...

UNIT 22
To Tell Of A DECISION

● **Key Structures**

1. Watashi wa kyō ano hito to au-koto ni shimasu.

2. Watashi wa rai-getsu Doitsu e iku-koto ni shimashita.

3. (Anata wa) kōhī to kō-cha no dochira ni shimasu ka?
   —Kō-cha ni shimasu.

4. Rai-nen kara Tōkyō ni sumu-koto ni narimashita.

---

1   N wa V·u-/V·nai-koto ni suru/kime·

     N decides to/not to do....

2   N wa [Something] ni suru/kime·

     N decides on [Something].

3   N wa V·u-/V·nai-koto ni nar·

     It is decided that N will/will not....

This Construction is used when circumstances have taken the decision out of N's hands and forced an action.

So far, we have followed convention and used 'Past' and 'Present' as grammatical terms. In fact, 'Perfect' and 'Imperfect' Aspects would be more descriptive of these Japanese functions. →FS

The shimashita, kimashita, and narimashita in 1, 2, and 3 are not so much past tense as they are 'Perfect Aspect.'

1. I'm determined to meet him today.

2. I've decided to go to Germany next month.

3. Which do you want, coffee or tea?

   —I'll have tea.

4. We're going to live in Tokyo beginning next year.

★More Examples For Practice

1 Kyō wa haya·ku kaeru-**koto ni shimasu**.

Kono ie o kau-**koto ni shimasu**.

Doitsu-go o narau-**koto ni shimashita**.

Tōkyō ni sumu-**koto ni kimemashita**.

Anata-gata wa kekkon-**suru-koto ni kimemashita** ka?

2 Watashi wa kono kamera o kau-koto ni shimasu. Anata wa?

—Watashi wa ano kamera **ni shimasu**.

Dore **ni shimasu** ka?

—Sono aka·i no **ni shimasu**.

Anata wa doko ni sumu tsumori desu ka?

—Kamakura **ni kimemashita**.

Itsu hikkosu tsumori desu ka?

—Kon-getsu no tō-ka **ni shimashita**.

3 Watashi-tachi wa rikon-**suru-koto ni narimashita**.

Rai-getsu Ōsaka ni tenkin-**suru-koto ni narimashita**. Anata to shibaraku awa**nai-koto ni narimasu**.

1 I think I'll go home early today.

We'll settle on buying this house.

I've made up my mind to study German.

We've decided to live in Tokyo.

Have you decided to get married?

2 I'll buy this camera. How about you?

—I'll take that one.

Which one do you want?

—That red one, please.

Where are you going to live?

—We've decided on Kamakura.

When do you plan to move there?

—On the tenth of this month.

3 We're going to get a divorce.

I'm going to be transferred to the Osaka office next month.

So I may not see you for some time.

● Further Study

Imperfect vs. Perfect

English has six tenses (past, present, future, and their respective perfects) while Japanese has only the two Aspects of Perfect and Imperfect. This alone shows that Japanese is based upon a system of time conceptualization quite different from English. The Japanese choice of the Perfect or Imperfect Aspect depends upon whether or not the event in question is completed—Perfect if it is and Imperfect if it is not. Thus the Perfect can occasionally be used even for future events. The correspondence between these Japanese Aspects and English tenses is roughly as shown below.

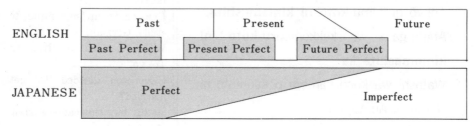

Let us take tabe· ⟨to eat⟩ as an example to compare the two.

I will eat	tabemasu
I will have eaten	tabete shimaimasu ⟨➡Unit 16 ②⟩
I eat	tabemasu
I have eaten	tabemashita
I have already eaten	tabete shimaimashita
I have once eaten	tabeta-koto ga arimasu ⟨➡Unit 17 ①⟩
I have been eating	tabete imashita/imasu ⟨➡Unit 16 ①⟩
I ate	tabemashita
I had eaten	tabemashita
I had already eaten	tabete shimaimashita
I had once eaten	tabeta-koto ga arimashita
I had been eating	tabete imashita

●Conversation

ZANNEN NAGARA. . . . ──《Calling The Company》

—Moshi-moshi, Ōsaka Denki desu ka?
  Yushutsu-bu bu-chō no Katō-san,
  o-negai-shimasu.

Katō desu ga. . . .

—Watashi wa Yū-esu Erekutorikku no
  Jon Sumisu desu. Ima Kyōto ni
  kite imasu. Getsu-yōbi made kochira
  ni iru tsumori desu.

  Ka-yōbi ni sochira e iku-koto ni
  shimasu ga, yoroshi·i desu ka?

I·i desu. O-denwa o matte imashita.

—Ka-yōbi, sha-chō-san ni au-koto ga
  dekimasu ka?

Zannen-nagara, sha-chō wa kinō kara
Tōkyō e shutchō-shite imasu.

Sui-yōbi ni kaeru hazu desu.

—Sore-dewa, Sui-yōbi no hō ga i·i
  kamo shiremasen ne.

Jā, sō shite kudasai. Sassoku, sha-
chō ni renraku-shimashō.

—O-negai shimasu. Ato-de mō ichi-do
  o-denwa-shimasu.

—Hello, Osaka Electric?
  May I have Mr. Kato,
  Director of the Export
  Department?
Kato speaking.
—I'm John Smith of U. S.
  Electric.   I'm now in
  Kyoto. I plan to be here
  until Monday.
  I'm supposed to go to your
  place on Tuesday.
  Is that OK?
Good. We've been waiting
for your call.
—On Tuesday, would I be
  able to meet your Presi-
  dent?
Unfortunately, he went to
Tokyo on business yester-
day.
He is to be back on Wednes-
day.
—Then, maybe Wednesday
  would be better.
In that case, please come on
Wednesday.
I'll get in touch with the
President right away.
—Thank you. I'll call you
  again later.

●Look & Learn

Nani ni shimasu ka?

⟨What would you like?⟩

sūpu   wain   bīru   jūsu

sutēki   katsu   karē-raisu

ebi-furai   hanbāgā   sarada

sakana   ebi   kani

bīfu   pōku   chikin

tamago   raisu   pan

New Words For UNIT 23

ao·i	blue; green
	Cf. ao blue/green color
Chikyū	the earth
dame	⟨Cph⟩ ⟨Na⟩ no good
darō	⟨Plain Form of deshō⟩
	→FS
Den-den-kōsha	Japan Telegraph and
	Telephone Corporation
	Cf. -kōsha Corporation
	e.g. Kōtsū-kōsha Japan
	Travel Bureau; Senbai-
	kōsha Japan Monopoly
	Corporation
denpō	telegraph
dewa	⟨Verbal Particle in Nega-
	tive⟩
	dewa arimasen am/is/are
	not →U-7 KS
	dewa arimasen deshita
	was/were not →U-10 KS
	dewa nai am/is/are not
	⟨Plain Form⟩ →FS
	dewa nakatta was/were
	not ⟨Plain Form⟩ →FS
Gagārin	Gagarin, Yurii Alekseye-
	vich ⟨Russian cosmonaut;
	1934–68⟩
garasu	⟨←Dutch *glas*⟩ glass ⟨the
	material⟩
	Cf. gurasu ←glass ⟨cup⟩
hagaki	postcard
hōsō-kyoku	broadcasting station
	hōsō ⟨Nv⟩ broadcast;
	-kyoku office, bureau

Itaria	⟨←Italian *Italia*⟩ Italy
itsu-demo	at any time →U-4 FS
iw·	to say
kaiwa	⟨Nv⟩ conversation
kane-mochi	richness, rich person
	kane metal; money
	Cf. o-kane money
	mochi ←mot·
kat·	to win, conquer, overcome
keiyaku	⟨Nv⟩ contract
(o-)kure	⟨Plain Form of kudasai⟩
	→FS
or·	=i· ⟨modest; used for
	First Person and his
	family, etc.⟩
saki-hodo	some time ago (=sakki)
Shīzā	Caesar, Julius ⟨100–44 B.C.⟩
shōjiki-na	honest
shuppan-sha	publishing company
	shuppan ⟨Nv⟩ publish
	-sha ...company, firm
shuppatsu	⟨Nv⟩ start
terekkusu	←telex
toranjisutā-rajio	←transistor radio
yasashi·i	easy; gentle, kind
yunyū	⟨Nv⟩ import
	Cf. yushutsu ⟨Nv⟩ export
zasshi	magazine

UNIT 23
To QUOTE Someone

● Key Structures

1. Kare wa "Do-yō(bi) ni shuppatsu-suru" to iimashita.

2. Kare wa Do-yō(bi) ni shuppatsu-suru to itte imasu.

3. (Anata wa) kore wa daiyamondo da to omoimasu ka?

   —Iie, garasu da to omoimasu.

4. Tanaka-san wa daiyamondo da to omotte imasu.

---

1 | **N wa** [Sentence] **to iimashita.** | N said, "[Sentence]."

2 | **N wa** [Sentence] **to itte imasu.** | N says, "[Sentence]."

In the Construction **2**, N can seldom be First Person or Second Person, since it would be strange to say, 'I say, "......"', wouldn't it? Thus Japanese rarely say Watashi wa "......" to itte imasu, or Anata wa "......" to itte imasu ka?

While Japanese does not make a clear distinction between direct and indirect quotations, speech is usually quoted as it was spoken, as in English direct quotation. Vᴾ/Plain Forms ⟨→FS⟩ are preferred in the subordinate [Sentence].

3 | **N wa** [Sentence] **to omow·** | N thinks [Sentence].

In this Construction, omow· takes the forms omotte imasu, omotte imashita, etc. rather than omoimasu, omoimashita, etc. when N is Third Person. Again, Vᴾ/Plain Forms ⟨→FS⟩ are preferred in the subordinate [Sentence].

1. He said, "I'll leave on Saturday."

2. He says he'll leave on Saturday.

3. Do you think this is a diamond?

   —No, I think it is glass.

4. Mr. Tanaka thinks this is a diamond.

★More Examples For Practice

1. Shīzā wa "Kita, mita, katta," **to iimashita**.

   So-ren no Gagārin wa "Chikyū wa ao·i," **to iimashita**.

   Watashi wa chichi ni, jidōsha ga hoshi·i **to iimashita**. Shikashi, chichi wa, dame da **to iimashita**.

2. Kare wa Yōroppa e iku **to itte imasu**. Kare wa Porutogaru-go wa muzukashi·i **to itte imasu**.

3. (Anata wa) Nippon-go wa muzukashi·i **to omoimasu** ka?

   —Iie, amari muzukashi·ku-na·i **to omoimasu**. Yasashi·i desu.

   (Anata wa) kare wa shōjiki da **to omoimasu** ka?

   —Hai, **sō omoimasu**.

   (Watashi wa) kare wa konai **to omoimasu**.

   Itaria-jin wa Nippon-jin wa kane-mochi da **to omotte imasu**.

1. Caesar said, "I came, I saw, I conquered." (*Veni, vidi, vici.*)
   Gagarin, the Russian cosmonaut, said, "The earth is blue."
   I told Father I wanted a car, but he told me no.
2. He says he is going to Europe.
   He says Portuguese is difficult.
3. Do you think Japanese is difficult?
   —No. I don't think it's so difficult. It's easy.
   Do you think he is honest?
   —Yes, I think so.
   I don't think he will come.
   Italians think that Japanese are rich.

●Further Study

Plain Forms

V^M is, in fact, the polite style of colloquial Japanese, while V^P is the frank or unadorned style. Accordingly, when you want to speak plainly, you can use the V^P forms instead of the V^M forms and occasionally put sentence-ending particles ⟨➡Unit 27 FS⟩ after V^P. Desu, deshita, etc. also have their respective Plain Forms as shown below.

I. Plain Forms of 'N/N(a) **desu**'

	Affirmative	Negative
Imperfect	N/N(a) da	N/N(a) dewa nai
Perfect	N/N(a) datta	N/N(a) dewa nakatta

NB: The interrogative form of 'N/N(a) da' is not 'N/N(a) da ka? but simply 'N/N(a) ka?'

II. Plain Forms of 'A·**i** **desu**'

	Affirmative	Negative
Imperfect	A·i	A·ku·na·i
Perfect	A·katta	A·ku·na·katta

NB: In effect, you simply leave off desu. Plain Forms other than those shown above are:

V·ō for V·mashō; N o (o-)kure for N o kudasai;
V·te/V·nai de for V·te/V·nai de kudasai; darō for deshō; and
ikenai/naranai/shirenai for ikemasen/narimasen/shiremasen

●Conversation

SORE WA YO·KATTA!——《Arranging The Visit》

—Katō-san desu ne. Jon Sumisu
  desu.

Saki-hodo wa o-denwa dōmo arigatō

gozaimashita. Sassoku Tōkyō no

sha-chō ni denwa-shimashita. Sha-

chō wa zehi anata ni o-ai-shitai to itte

orimasu. Sui-yōbi no nan-ji goro ga

yoroshi·i deshō ka?

—Itsu-demo i·i desu.

Jā, san-ji ni kimemashō.

　　　　*　*　*

—Moshi-moshi, Tanaka Kaoru-san

  desu ka? Jon desu.

  Ototoi kara Kyōto ni imasu.

Ōsaka Denki niwa itsu iku-koto ni

narimashita ka?

—Sui-yōbi no gogo ni sha-chō-san ni

  au-koto ni narimashita.

  Toranjisutā-rajio no yunyū no

  keiyaku ga dekiru to omoimasu.

Sore wa yo·katta desu ne.

—Mr. Kato? I'm John Smith.
Thank you for your call.
I immediately got in touch
with our boss. He said he
definitely wants to meet you.
What time on Wednesday
will be convenient for you?
—Any time would be fine.
Then let's make it at three
o'clock.
　　　*　*　*
—Hello, Kaoru Tanaka?
  This is John.
  I've been in Kyoto since
  the day before yesterday.
When are you going to
visit Osaka Electric?
—It's been arranged that I'm
  going to meet the Presi-
  dent Wednesday afternoon.
  I think I'll be able to get
  the import contract for
  the transistor radios.
That's good.

▼A festival in Kyoto

●Look & Learn

Communication Media

shinbun

zasshi

terebi

rajio

Media Companies

shinbun-sha
〈newspaper company〉

shuppan-sha
〈publisher〉

hōsō-kyoku
〈broadcasting station〉

Den-den-kōsha
〈Telegraph & Telephone
Corporation〉

denwa

denpō

hagaki

tegami

terekkusu

kaiwa
〈conversation〉

New Words For UNIT 24

aini in order to meet ←aw·
→KS

arenji 〈Nv〉 ←arrange

arubaito 〈Nv〉 〈←German *Arbeit*〉
side job; part-time job

byūtifuru-na ←beautiful

dēto 〈Nv〉 ← date

dōzo please
Dōzo. 〈Cph〉 Please (come
in).; Here it is.; Why not?
Dōzo yoroshi·ku. 〈Cph〉
Pleased to meet you.

go-zonji desu ka? 〈Cph〉 Do you know
...? 〈Polite〉

ikaga 〈Cph〉 How...?
e.g. Tenpura wa ikaga?
How would you like tem-
pura?
Okā-san no go-byōki wa
ikaga desu ka? How is
your mother's illness?

Ikeda 〈family name〉

intānashonaru-na ←international

iroiro-na various

jikan time

Jitsu-wa, In fact,; To tell the truth,

kaimono 〈Nv〉 shopping

...kara after (doing)... →U-28 KS

kekkon-shiki wedding
kekkon 〈Nv〉 marry
shiki ceremony

kontakuto 〈Nv〉 ←contact

kyatchi 〈Nv〉 ←catch

Maikeru Fokkusu ←Michael Fox

Maiku ←Mike

modan-na ←modern

...ni with a view to...

o-jikan (your) time (to spare for
me)
Jikan ga arimasen. I am
busy.
O-jikan ga arimasu ka?
Do you have the time (to
spare me)?

romanchikku-na ←romantic

shinagara while doing... →KS

tor· to take; bring [Something]
→p. 83

Wārudo Erekutorikku ←World Electric

wasure· to forget

Yamada 〈family name〉

yor· to approach
...ni yor· to drop in;
stop over

Boku and Kimi

In addition to watashi and anata,
Japanese has many Pronouns meaning 'I' and 'you.' Someone once
counted over 50 Pronouns for 'I'
alone. Each individual chooses the
Pronoun to suit his own style, posi-
tion, and occasion. But the most
commonly used for informal conversation among men are boku 〈I〉 and
kimi 〈you〉. These, however, are
distinctly masculine forms and
would not be used by women.

UNIT 24
To Indicate PURPOSE

● Key Structures

1. Watashi wa koko e anata ni aini kimashita.

2. Tanaka-san wa kōen e sanpo ni ikimashita.

3. Watashi wa kono eiga o mite kaerimasu.

4. Tabako o katte kimashō ka?

|||||||||||||||||||||||||||||||||||||||||||||||||||||||||||||||||||||||||||||||||||||||||||||||||||

1 | V·ni ik·/kuru/kaer· | go/come/return to do. . .

For how to make V·ni forms, ➡FS.

2 | N ni ik·/kuru/kaer· | go/come/return for (doing) N

Do you remember the Verbal Nouns V^c·i/V^v ⟨➡Unit 18 FS I. (3)⟩?
Since V·ni in [1] is V^c·ini or V^v·ni, it can be replaced by 'N ni.'

3 | V·te ik·/kuru/kaer· | go/come/return after doing. . .

V·te being like '~ing,' this Construction means, 'to go/come/return ~ing.' Cf. [1]

Already, we have seen some ways to combine words, such as N+N ⟨➡Unit 1⟩. So you may be wondering how to combine two V's. Use 'V·te V.' As for Na/A+Na/A ➡Unit 27 [3].

'V_1·te V_2' can mean two things: ① V_1 and V_2 at the same time or ② V_2 after V_1. Thus [3] can mean either 'go etc. ~ing' ⟨➡Unit 9 [5]⟩ or 'go etc. after ~ing.' If you want to mean Situation ② explicitly, use 'V_1·te kara V_2.' If you want to mean Situation ① explicitly, you can use 'V_1·nagara V_2.' In this case, the V_1 forms are V^v·nagara, V^c·inagara, and shinagara.

1. I've come here to meet you.

2. Mr. Tanaka went to the park for a walk.

3. I'll see this film and then go home.

4. Shall I go buy some cigarettes?

★More Examples For Practice

☐ Ashita depāto e wai-shatsu o kai**ni ikimasu**.

Hiru-gohan o tabe**ni ikimashō** ka?

Eiga o mi**ni ikitai** desu.

Nippon e benkyō-**shini kimashita**.

Yamada-san wa kaban o wasuremashita.

Ima (ie e) tori**ni kaerimashita**.

☐ Shokuji **ni ikimashō** ka?

Eiga **ni ikitai** desu.

Nippon e benkyō **ni kimashita**.

Jon-san wa imōto-san no kekkon-shiki **ni**

Amerika e **kaerimashita**.

Kaimono **ni ikimasen** ka?

☐ Koko de shokuji o **shite kaerimasu**.

Tabako o kat**te kite** kudasai.

Gohan o tabe**te kimashita** ka?

—Iie, mada desu.

Watashi no imōto no apāto wa koko

desu. Chotto yot**te ikimasen** ka?

☐ I'll go to the department store to buy a dress shirt tomorrow.
Shall we go have lunch?
I want to go and see the film.
I came to Japan to study.
Yamada forgot to bring his bag.
He has gone home to get it.
☐ Shall we go for something to eat?
I want to go to a film.
I came to Japan to study.
John went back to America for his sister's wedding.
Why don't we go shopping?
☐ I'll have something to eat here and I'll go home/before I go home.
Please go buy some cigarettes.
Have you eaten your lunch?
—No, not yet.
This is my sister's apartment.
Why don't we visit her for a while?

● Further Study

How to Make V•ni Forms

Cf. V•masu ➡Unit 8 FS

I. V^v ⟨Vowel-ending Verbs⟩

$$V^v + \boxed{\text{ni}}$$

e.g. tabe•→ tabe**ni**

oki• → oki**ni**

II. V^c ⟨Consonant-ending Verbs⟩ Cf. Sound Law ⟨1⟩ ➡Unit 8 FS

$$V^c + \boxed{\text{i}} + \boxed{\text{ni}}$$

e.g. kak• → kak**ini**

yom•→ yom**ini**

mat• → ma**chini**

aw• → a**ini**

III. V^x ⟨Irregular Verbs⟩

suru ⟶ **shini**

NB: There is no V•ni form for kuru.

Japanization of Foreign Words

We have Japanized quite a number of foreign words and are creating more new (?) words every day. Not only do we make Na out of English adjectives, such as intānashonaru-na ⟨international⟩, byūtifuru-na ⟨beautiful⟩, romanchikku-na ⟨romantic⟩, and modan-na ⟨modern⟩; but we also make Nv out of all manner of foreign words. For example, there are kyatchi-suru ⟨to catch⟩, kontakuto-suru ⟨to contact⟩, dēto-suru ⟨to date⟩, arenji-suru ⟨to arrange⟩, arubaito-suru ⟨to have a side job⟩, and many more.

To confuse you still further, we pronounce these as though they were really Japanese and sometimes even abbreviate these borrowed words.

●Conversation

KOCHIRA WA SHA-CHŌ——《Visiting The Company》

Kochira wa sha-chō no Ikeda desu.

Kochira, Yū-esu Erekutorikku no Jon

Sumisu-san desu.

——Hajimemashite.

—Sumisu desu. Dōzo yoroshi·ku.

——Kyōto wa ikaga deshita ka?

—Yo·katta desu. Iroiro-na o-tera ya

　jinja o mite kimashita.

——Sore wa yo·katta desu ne.

　　Tokoro-de, Wārudo Erekutorikku

　　no Maikeru Fokkusu-san o go-zonji

　　desu ka?

—Ē, yo·ku shitte imasu.

——Jitsu-wa, Tōkyō de Fokkusu-san

　　to atte kimashita.

—Sō desu ka? Maiku wa mō Nippon ni

　kite imasu ka? Nippon e terebi no

　keiyaku ni iku to itte imashita ga....

Asu o-jikan ga arimasu ka?

—Hai, gozaimasu.

Sore-ja, zehi kōjō mo mite kaette

kudasai.

This is our President, Mr. Ikeda.
This is Mr. John Smith of U. S. Electric.
——How do you do?
—My name is Smith. Glad to meet you.
——How did you like Kyoto?
—Very nice. I saw a lot of temples and shrines.
——That's nice.
　By the way, do you know Mr. Michael Fox of World Electric?
—Yes, I know him very well.
——In fact, I met Mr. Fox in Tokyo.
—Did you? Is Mike here already? He said he was coming to Japan for a television contract.
Are you free tomorrow?
—Yes, I am.
If so, please look around our factory before you return to Tokyo.

▼Keihin industrial area

●Look & Learn

On My/Your Way

Watashi wa ________•ni ikimasu. 〈I'll go to do ________.〉
Anata wa ________•te kaerimasu ka?
〈Will you do ________ on your way home?〉

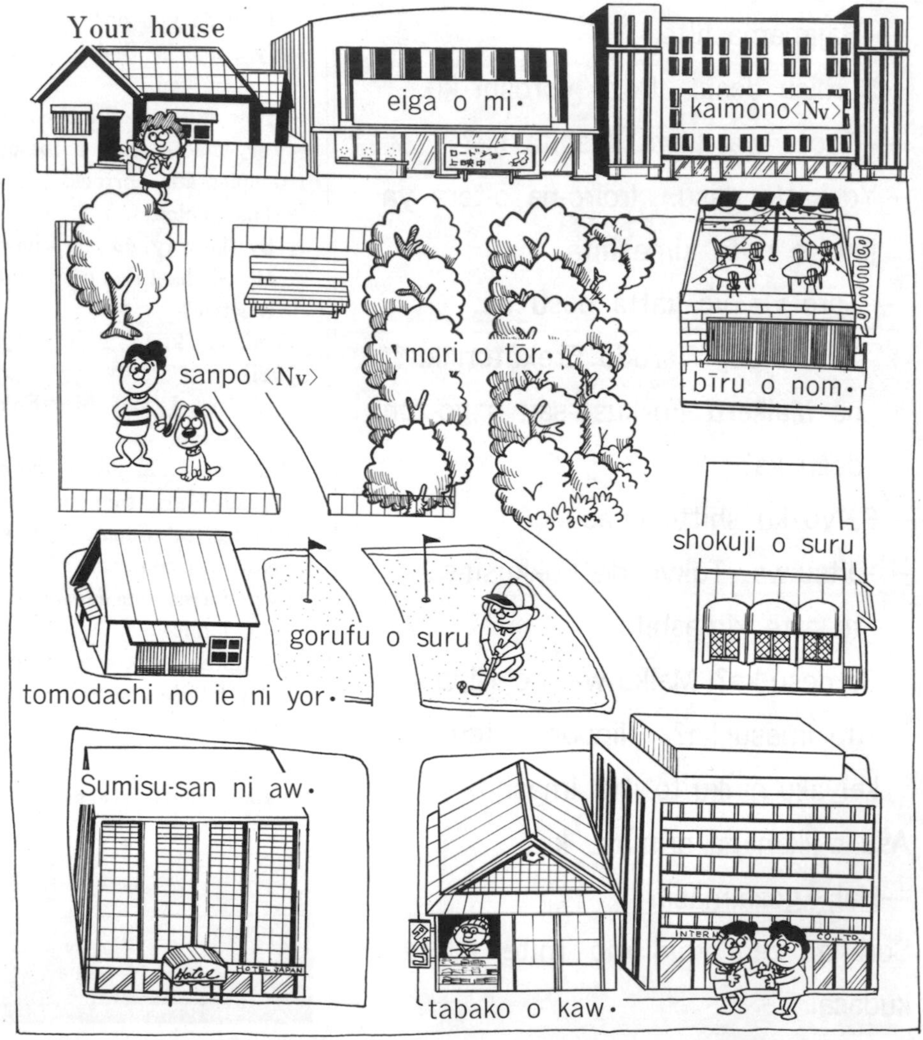

Your house
eiga o mi•
kaimono〈Nv〉
ロードショー
上映中
sanpo 〈Nv〉
mori o tōr•
bīru o nom•
shokuji o suru
gorufu o suru
tomodachi no ie ni yor•
Sumisu-san ni aw•
Hotel
HOTEL JAPAN
INTER
CO.LTD.
tabako o kaw•

New Words For UNIT 25

aida	⟨N⟩ between, during, space →p. 179
batan	bang ⟨sound of a door as it is closed⟩
bōeki	⟨Nv⟩ foreign trade
bū-bū	⟨hooting/honking sound⟩
chikku-takku	tick-tock ⟨sound of a clock⟩
gachan	⟨sound of crashing, breaking⟩
go-yō	errand, business (=yō)
gū-gū	Zzzz...
ik·	to go ⟨V·te form: itte⟩ ...e/ni ik· to go to... ...o ik· to go along...
kado	corner ⟨seen from outside⟩ Cf. sumi corner ⟨seen from inside⟩

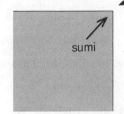

← kado

sumi

kanban	signboard, billboard
kangae	thought, idea Cf. kangae· to think →U-18 FS I. (3)
kikoe·	to be audible →KS
kimochi	feeling
kīn	⟨sound of a jet airplane flying⟩
koe	voice
koke-kokkō	cock-a-doodle-doo
kon-kon	⟨sound of someone knocking at the door⟩
kuro·i	black

	Cf. kuro black color
massugu	⟨N(a)/Adv⟩ straight
mie·	to be visible →KS
mizu-umi	lake mizu water; umi sea Cf. ike pond
nyā-nyā	meow
ogyā-ogyā	⟨crying of a baby⟩
ongaku	music Cf. ongaku-ka musician
oto	sound
saisho	⟨N⟩ the first
sentā	←center
Sumimasen	ga, ⟨Cph⟩ Excuse me, but...
-to	⟨Suffix to derive Adv from onomatopoetic/mimetic words⟩
urusa·i	noisy, annoying
wakar·	to be perceptible ...ga wakar· to understand →KS
wan-wan	bow-wow
yane	roof
yō	errand, business (=yōji)

yane

okujō

TAPE ②-Ⓑ

● Key Structures

1. Anata wa Nippon-go ga wakarimasu ka?
    —Hai, sukoshi wakarimasu.
2. Anata wa asu koko e kimasu ka?
    —Wakarimasen.
3. Koko kara Fuji-san ga miemasu.
4. Tonari no heya kara kirei-na ongaku ga kikoemasu.

---

1 | **N wa [Something] ga wakar·** | N understands [Something].

'To know' is expressed by shitte i· ⟨➡Unit 16 ①⟩. Shitte i·, however, means 'to have a knowledge (of...)' and, strictly speaking, it is slightly different from 'to know.' Being asked, "Do you plan to come tomorrow?", you may answer in English, "I don't know." But in Japanese you would not say, "Shirimasen" ⟨➡Unit 16 FS⟩, because it is unnatural to have no knowledge of your own intentions. Instead, you would say Wakarimasen—wakar· meaning 'to be perceptible/noticeable/analyzable/understandable.' You cannot say '[Something] o wakar·.' It is '[Something] ga wakar·.' This Construction ① literally means, 'For N, [Something] is analyzable/understandable.'

2 | N (ni)wa [Something] ga $\begin{cases} \text{mie·} \\ \text{kikoe·} \end{cases}$ | N $\begin{cases} \text{sees} \\ \text{hears} \end{cases}$ [Something].

Mie· means 'to be visible,' and kikoe· 'to be audible.' Compare these to mi· meaning 'to watch/look (at)' and kik·, 'to listen (to).'

1. Do you understand Japanese?

   —Yes, a little.

2. Are you coming tomorrow?

   —I don't know.

3. You can see Mt. Fuji from here.

4. Beautiful music is audible from the next room.

★More Examples For Practice

1 Anata **wa** Ei-go **ga wakarimasu** ka?

   —Iie, zenzen **wakarimasen**.

   Watashi **wa** Tōkyō Eki ga **wakarimasen**.

   —Watashi mo **wakarimasen**.

   (Watashi **wa**) anata no kangae ga **wakarimasen**.

   (Watashi **wa**) anata no kimochi **ga** yo·ku **wakarimasu**.

   Igirisu-jin wa, Nippon-jin **wa** inu no kimochi **ga wakarana·i** to omotte imasu.

2 Watashi no heya no mado kara Tōkyō Tawā **ga miemasu**.

   Ano kanban **ga miemasu** ka?

   Mizu-umi no mukō ni mori **ga miemasu**.

   Hikō-ki kara Fuji-san **ga miemashita** ka?

   —Hai, yo·ku **miemashita**.

   Hora, taki no oto **ga kikoemasu**.

   Kotori no koe mo **kikoemasu**.

   Yo·ku **kikoemasen**.

---

1 Do you understand English?

—No, not at all.
I don't know where Tokyo Station is.
—I don't know either.
I don't understand what you are thinking.
I know just how you feel.
English people think Japanese don't understand dogs' feelings.

2 I can see Tokyo Tower from my window.
Do you see that signboard?
Beyond the lake is seen the forest.
Could you see Mt. Fuji from your airplane?
—Yes, very clearly.
Listen, we hear the sound of the waterfall.
We hear birds chirping, too.
I can't hear you very well.

● Further Study

SUMMARY OF HOMONYMOUS POSTPOSITIONALS

⟨Preceded by⟩		⟨Followed by⟩	
ato			U-29 ⑤
[Group/Place]/naka/uchi			U-15 ③
N/N(a)	**de**		U-27 ③④
[Place]			U-9 ②
[Something]			U-9 ①
V·nai		kudasai	U-12 ③

hō			U-15 ①, U-20 ④⑤
N/-koto/-no	**ga**		{ U-19 ③FS, U-26 FS, U-30 FS
[Sentence]		[Sentence]	U-28 ④

[Place/Time]/[Person]			U-5 ③, U-11 ①
[Sentence]	**kara**		U-28 ①②
V·te			U-24 ③

aida/mae			U-29 ③④
[Person]			U-11 ①②③
[Place]			U-3 ③④, U-5 ①②
[Time]	**ni**		{ U-6 ②, U-17 FS III, U-29 ①② FS
		chigaina·i	U-14 ④
		suru/kime·/nar·	{ U-22 ①②③, U-27 ①②
		ik·/kaer·/kuru	U-5 ②, U-24 ②

N			U-9 ③
N		N	U-1 ②, U-15 ①③
[Sentence]	**to**	iw·	U-23 ①②
[Sentence]		omow·	U-21 ②, U-23 ③

●Conversation

SUMIMASEN GA. . . .————————《Asking The Way》

—Sumimasen ga, Bōeki Sentā wa
   doko deshō ka?
E? Watashi wa Ei-go ga wakarimasen.
—Watashi wa Nippon-go de hanashite
   imasu ga. . . .
E? Ā, sō desu ka? Nan no go-yō
desu ka?
—Bōeki Sentā o sagashite imasu.
   Shirimasen ka?
Bōeki Sentā. . .? Ā, shitte imasu.
Asoko ni, hora, kuro·i biru ga
miemasu ne. Sono migi-gawa no
michi o massugu ikimasu.
—Chotto matte kudasai. Ano aka·i
   yane no ie to kuro·i biru no aida
   no michi desu ka?
Sō desu. Soshite, saisho no kado o
hidari ni magarimasu.
Sugu wakarimasu yo.
—Dōmo arigatō.
Iie.

—Excuse me, but where is
the Trade Center?
Pardon? I don't understand
English.
—I'm speaking in Japanese.
Oh, you are? What do you
want?
—I'm looking for the Trade
Center. Do you know
where it is?
The Trade Center? Yes, I
know. Over there, look, you
see that black building, don't
you? Go straight along the
road to the right of that
building.
—Wait a moment. You mean
the street between that
house with the red roof
and the black building?
Right. Then turn left at the
first corner. You can't miss
it.
—Thank you.
Not at all.

▼Tokyo World Trade Center

●Look & Learn

Sounds And Noises Everywhere

Wan-wan!

Gachan!

Chikku-takku!

Kīn!

Bū-bū!

Urusa·i!

Gū-gū.....

Nyā-nyā!

Ogyā-ogyā!

Kon-kon!

Batan!

Koke-kokkō!

NB : These can be used as Adverbs by putting -to after them.

New Words For UNIT 26

antena	←antenna
ar·	to exist, stay, be
	...ga ar· ① There be...
	⟨Inanimate⟩ →U-3
	② to have... →KS
	V·ta-koto ga ar· →U-17
atama	head
chigaw·	to differ
	Chigaimasu. ⟨Cph⟩ No,
	not that.
efu-emu	←FM
gan-ka	ophthalmology
ge-ka	surgery
ha	tooth
hana	nose
hara	belly, stomach
heso	navel
hi	daytime; the sun
ita·i	painful, sore →LL
jibiinkō-ka	ear, nose, and throat sec-
	tion, ENT department
jinkō	population
josei	woman
	Cf. dansei man
-jū	all over/through...
kami (no ke)	hair ⟨on the scalp⟩
ke	hair; feathers; fur
kuchi	mouth
me	eye
mimi	ear
moderu	←model
mune	chest, bosom
musume	daughter; young girl
	→U-7 LL
nai-ka	internal medicine
nami	wave
Naruhodo.	⟨Cph⟩ I see.; Indeed.
...niwa	→KS
nodo	throat

ō·i	many, much, plenty
	⟨this is used only as a
	Predicative; to modify N,
	it should be ō·ku no.
	Some other Adjectives like
	this are: chika·i/chika·ku
	no near;
	tō·i/tōku no far.⟩
okur·	to send
onaka	stomach
otō-san	father →U-7 LL
purasuchikku	←plastic
sanfujin-ka	obstetrics and gynecology
sanpuru	←sample
se	back ⟨of the body⟩
	se ga taka·i tall
	se ga hiku·i short
-sei	made in/by...
seihin	product, manufactured
	goods
seishin-ka	psychiatrics
sekai	world
sekai-jū	⟨N⟩ all over the world
seki	⟨Nv⟩ cough
	seki ga de· to cough
shi-ka	dentistry
supīkā	←(loud) speaker
tanpa	short wave ⟨radio⟩
tsuma	wife →U-7 LL
tsume	nail; claw
ude	arm
usagi	rabbit
yogore·	to get dirty
yubi	finger; toe

UNIT 26
To Give A DETAILED Description

● Key Structures

1. Kono kamera wa renzu ga purasuchikku desu.

2. Keiko-san wa me ga kirei desu.

3. Watashi wa atama ga ita·i desu.

4. Kono ningyō wa te ga ugokimasu.

5. Watashi (ni)wa otōto ga arimasu.

<hr>

1 $\boxed{\text{N}_1 \textbf{ wa } [\text{Detail/Part}] \textbf{ ga } \text{N}_2/\text{N(a)}/\text{A·i desu.}}$

2 $\boxed{\textbf{N wa } [\text{Part}] \textbf{ ga } \text{V}^{\text{M}}}$

First say 'N wa' to draw the listener's attention to what you are to describe, specify the point/detail/part of N with ga, and then complete your description. These Constructions are used when you want to make a statement about N as a whole, choosing some point/detail/part/attribute as representative of N.

3 $\boxed{\text{N}_1 \textbf{ (ni)wa } \text{N}_2 \textbf{ ga } \textbf{ar·/i·}}$ N_1 has N_2.

Obviously, this Construction is based on the same premise as ⓵ and ⓶. This is used when N_1 'has' N_2 in the English usage, although N_1 cannot 'own/possess/hold in the hand' N_2. For example, when you say, "I have a brother," you cannot be the owner of your brother, neither are you actually holding your brother in your hands. This is when you use this Construction 〈'With N_1, N_2 exists.'〉.

When N_2 is animate, i· as well as ar· is used. Cf. Unit 3 ③.

1. This camera has a plastic lens.

2. Keiko has beautiful eyes.

3. I have a headache.

4. The arms of this doll move.

5. I have a younger brother.

★More Examples For Practice

1 Usagi **wa** me **ga** aka·i desu.

　Jon-san **wa** kami **ga** naga·i desu.

　Sumisu-san **wa** atama **ga** i·i desu.

　Ano hito **wa** se **ga** taka·i desu.

　Nippon **wa** jinkō **ga** ō·i desu.

　Fuyu **wa** hi **ga** mijika·i desu.

　Fuyu no umi **wa** nami **ga** taka·i desu.

　Anata **wa** ha **ga** kirei desu.

　Ano hito **wa** otō-san **ga** yūmei desu.

　Ano hito **wa** oji-san **ga** seiji-ka desu.

　Watashi no ie **wa** tonari **ga** hon-ya desu.

　Kono kaisha **wa** sha-chō **ga** josei desu.

2 Yamada-san **wa** musume-san **ga** kyonen

　kekkon-shimashita.

　Watashi **wa** kodomo **ga** kotoshi daigaku

　ni hairimasu.

　Tōkyō **wa** kawa **ga** yogorete imasu.

3 Watashi (**ni**)**wa** tsuma **ga** arimasu.

　Watashi-tachi (**ni**)**wa** kodomo **ga** arima-

　sen.

1 A rabbit has red eyes.
John has long hair.
Smith is clever.
That person is tall.
Japan has a large population.
Winter days are short.
Waves are high on the winter sea.
You have beautiful teeth.
That person has a famous father.
That person's uncle is a politician.
There is a bookstore next to my house.
This company has a woman president.
2 Yamada has a daughter who got married last year.
My son/daughter will enter college this year.
The rivers in Tokyo are dirty.
3 I have a wife.
We don't have any children.

● Further Study

Summary of N **wa**... **ga**... Constructions

I. | N₁ **wa** N₂ **ga** |

ar・/i・ ⟨V⟩	➡ U-26 ③
deki・ ⟨V⟩	➡ U-18 ②
mie・/kikoe・ ⟨V⟩	➡ U-25 ②
wakar・ ⟨V⟩	➡ U-25 ①
jōzu/heta ⟨N(a)⟩	➡ U-18 ④
suki/kirai ⟨N(a)⟩	➡ U-20 ②
hoshi・i ⟨A・i⟩	➡ U-20 ③
hajimete ⟨N⟩	➡ U-19 ②
other N/N(a)/A・i	➡ U-26 ①
other V	➡ U-26 ②

II. | N **wa** V・ta-koto **ga** |

ar・ ⟨V⟩	➡ U-17 ①

III. | N **wa** V・u-koto **ga** |

deki・ ⟨V⟩	➡ U-18 ①

IV. | N **wa** V・u-no **ga** |

jōzu/heta ⟨N(a)⟩	➡ U-18 ③
suki/kirai ⟨N(a)⟩	➡ U-20 ①
hajimete ⟨N⟩	➡ U-19 ①

●Conversation

Ē, MOCHIRON.————— 《Signing The Contract》

Kore ga atarashi·i moderu desu.

—Naruhodo. Jitsu-wa, kinō Bōeki
  Sentā de kono seihin o mite
  kimashita.

I·i rajio deshō?

—Kono rajio wa tanpa ga hairimasu
  ka?

Ē, mochiron. Sekai-jū no tanpa o
kyatchi-shimasu. Efu-emu mo hairimasu
yo.

—Kore wa supīkā ga Igirisu-sei desu
  ka?

Iie, chigaimasu. Supīkā mo uchi de
tsukutte imasu.

—Kono rajio niwa antena ga
  arimasen ne?

Iie, arimasu yo. Hora, kore desu.

—Ā, naruhodo.

       *   *   *

—Jā, kono sanpuru o Nyū-yōku e
  okutte kudasai. Tabun kore o
  yunyū-suru-koto ni naru to
  omoimasu.

This is our new model.
—I see. To tell you the
  truth, I saw this at the
  Trade Center yesterday.
Good radio, isn't it?
—Does this radio get short
  wave?
Yes, of course. This catches
short wave from all over the
world. It gets FM, too.
—Is the speaker made in
  England?
No. We make the speakers
here, too.
—This radio doesn't have an
  antenna, does it?
Yes, it does. Look, here.
—Oh, I see.

       *   *   *

—Well, will you send a sam-
  ple of this to New York?
  I think we'll end up im-
  porting this model.

(Courtesy of Matsushita Electric
Industrial Co., Ltd.)

●Look & Learn

Parts Of Your Body

atama

hana

ha

nodo

mune

ashi

tsume

kami(no ke)

me

mimi

kuchi

ude

heso

yubi

te

onaka/hara

♦ **How to tell the doctor where it hurts:**

Watashi wa _____ ga ita·i desu.

♦ **Where to go in the hospital**

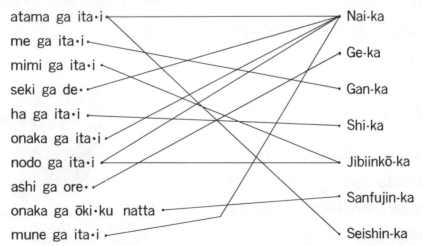

atama ga ita·i

me ga ita·i

mimi ga ita·i

seki ga de·

ha ga ita·i

onaka ga ita·i

nodo ga ita·i

ashi ga ore·

onaka ga ōki·ku natta

mune ga ita·i

Nai-ka

Ge-ka

Gan-ka

Shi-ka

Jibiinkō-ka

Sanfujin-ka

Seishin-ka

New Words For UNIT 27

akaru·i	light, bright
	Cf. kura·i dark
ama·i	sweet
	ama·kute sweet and →KS
-chō	head of... →LL
	e.g. sha-chō president of
	a company; eki-chō station
	master; kō-chō school prin-
	cipal; gaku-chō president
	of a university
daiji-na	important
...de	..., and →KS
furanku-na	←frank
gaku-chō	president of a college or
	university →LL
...gurai	about...
	Cf. ...goro about [Time]
hira(-sha-in)	mere clerk, employee
hontō	truth
	hontō no... true...
jo-kyōju	associate professor →LL
joshu	assistant →LL
ka-chō	section chief →LL
kakari-chō	chief clerk →LL
kindai-teki-na	modern
	kindai modern age
kitana·i	dirty, polluted
kokusai-teki-na	international
kōshi	lecturer →LL
kyōju	professor →LL
musuko	son →U-7 LL
nar·	to become; result (in)
	A·ku nar· to become A
	→KS
	...ni nar· to become...
	→KS
	V·u-/V·nai-koto ni nar·
	→U-22
nemu·i	sleepy

...nodesu	→FS
o-shigoto	(your) business (=shigoto)
sen-	last...
	sen-shū last week
	sen-getsu last month
sha-in	employee of a company
	Cf. kaisha-in company em-
	ployee ⟨as an occupation⟩
	e.g. Watashi wa kaisha-in
	desu. Gakken no sha-in
	desu.
shigoto	business, work, job
sora	sky, heaven
suru	① to do ② to play (sport)
	③ to decide ④ ⟨Suffix to
	make V out of Nv⟩ ⑤ to
	make →KS
	...o suru to do/play...
	...ni suru to decide on...
	→U-22
	N-suru to do N
	N_1 o N_2/N(a) ni suru
	→KS
	N o A·ku suru →KS
-teki-na	⟨Suffix to make Na⟩ -like
uma·i	delicious; nice; success-
	ful; skillful
	uma·ku ik· to go well,
	work out nicely, succeed
zutto	all the way/time; by far
	~-er
	X wa Y yori zutto ōki·i
	desu. X is much bigger
	than Y.

TAPE ②-Ⓑ

● Key Structures

1. Watashi wa shōrai isha ni narimasu.

2. Watashi wa nemu・ku narimashita.

3. Chichi wa watashi o isha ni shimashita.

4. Kono meron wa ama・kute oishi・i desu.

5. Emirī-san ga piano o hiite, Biru-san ga uta o utaimasu.

1 　N_1 **wa** N_2 **ni**/$N(a)$-**ni**/A・**ku** **nar**・　　N_1 becomes N_2/Na/A.

Nar・ means 'to become.' It is preceded by the Adverbial forms of A/ Na ⟨→Unit 9 ④⟩ or 'N ni.'

2 　N_1 **wa** N_2 **o** N_3 **ni**/$N(a)$-**ni**/A・**ku** **suru.**

N_1 makes N_2 N_3/Na/A.

3 　$\left.\begin{matrix} A_1 \\ Na_1 \end{matrix}\right\} + \left\{\begin{matrix} A_2 \\ Na_2 \end{matrix}\right. \longrightarrow \left.\begin{matrix} A_1・\textbf{ku(te)} \\ N(a)_1 \textbf{ de} \end{matrix}\right\} + \left\{\begin{matrix} A_2 \\ Na_2 \end{matrix}\right.$

This shows how to combine two Adjectives.

4 　$[\text{Sentence}_1] + [\text{Sentence}_2] \longrightarrow \left.\begin{matrix} \textbf{V・te} \\ \left.\begin{matrix} N \\ N(a) \end{matrix}\right\} \textbf{ de} \\ \Lambda・\textbf{ku(te)} \end{matrix}\right\} + [\text{Sentence}_2]$

When you want to combine two sentences, change the final part of the first sentence as shown.

1. I'll become a doctor in the future.

2. I got sleepy.

3. Father made me a doctor.

4. This melon is sweet and delicious.

5. Emily plays the piano, and Bill sings.

★More Examples For Practice

1 Tōkyō no sora wa kitana·**ku narima-shita**.

Ōsaka no machi wa kirei-**ni narimashita**.

Sen-getsu kare wa byōki **ni narimashita**.

—Mō genki-**ni narimashita** ka?

Anata wa nani **ni naritai** desu ka?

—Sensei **ni naritai** desu.

2 Watashi wa anata **o** shiawase-**ni shimasu**.

Nippon-jin wa inu **o** daiji-**ni shimasu**.

Heya **o** kirei-**ni shite kudasai**.

Heya **o** atataka·**ku shite kudasai**.

Shizuka-**ni shite kudasai**.

Watashi wa musuko **o** isha **ni suru** tsumori deshita. Shikashi, musuko wa ga-ka ni narimashita.

3 Kono heya wa hiro·**kute** akaru·i desu.

Ano hito wa shinsetsu **de** shōjiki desu.

4 Watashi wa Tōkyō e it**te**, Tanaka-san ni au tsumori desu.

Usagi wa mimi ga naga·**kute**, me ga aka·i desu.

1 The sky has become dirty in Tokyo.
The streets of Osaka have become clean.
He got ill last month.
—Has he recovered now?
What do you want to be?
—I want to be a teacher.
2 I'll make you happy.
Japanese take good care of dogs.
Clean the room, please.
Make the room warm, please.
Be quiet.
I wanted to make my son a doctor, but he became a painter.
3 This room is spacious and light.
He is kind and honest.
4 I plan to go to Tokyo and meet Tanaka there.
A rabbit has long ears and red eyes.

● Further Study

Sentence-ending Particles & Forms

Colloquial Japanese has some special particles and forms to end sentences. Some of these that are used in 'plain' speaking are listed below. Be careful, however, because there is a clear distinction between those used by men and those used by women.

Form of V etc. Preceding Particle or Form	Particles & Forms		Meaning or Function
	Masculine	Feminine	
V^M/V^P/desu/Plain Forms → Unit 23 FS	yo	wa	Calling particular attention to the statements
	ne	wane	Asking the listener's agreement
V^P/N/N(a)/A·i	darō?	deshō?	
V^P/Plain Forms → NB (2)	kai? → NB (3)		=ka? → Unit 4 □
V^P/N na-/Na/A·i		no?	
	n'da → NB (4)	no	Explaining the reasons, causes, circumstances, etc.

NB: (1) In Colloquial Japanese, V^M and desu are very often followed by yo or wa, which, in this case, may have no particular meaning. Instead of da yo by men, simply yo alone is used by women.

(2) If followed by kai?, da is omitted. Cf. Unit 23 FS I. NB

(3) When kai? is preceded by an Interrogative, dai? is used instead of kai?

(4) **N'da** is a Plain Form of nodesu/n'desu which has the same conjugational forms as desu.

●Conversation

NARUHODO.... ——————— 《Tokyo vs. Osaka》

O-shigoto wa uma·ku ikimashita ka?

—Hai, okage-sama-de.

Ōsaka wa dō deshita ka?

—Taihen yo·katta desu.

Sō desu ka?

—Ē, Ōsaka no hito wa Tōkyō no

hito yori zutto shinsetsu de,

furanku da to omoimasu.

Sō desu ka? Demo, machi wa

kitana·i deshō?

—Iie, sō wa omoimasen. Tōkyō wa itsu

Nippon no shuto ni natta nodesu

ka?

Yon-hyaku-nen gurai mae desu ga....

—Naruhodo.... Watashi wa Kyōto

ya Ōsaka e itte, hontō no Nippon

ga yo·ku wakarimashita.

Tōkyō wa kokusai-teki de kindai-

teki-na tokai desu.

Shikashi, Tōkyō niwa Nippon ga

arimasen ne.

Sō deshō ka?

Did your business go well?
—Yes, thank you.
Did you enjoy your trip to Osaka?
—Yes, very much.
Really?
—Yes. I think people are much kinder and franker in Osaka than they are in Tokyo.
Really? But the town is very dirty, isn't it?
—No, I don't think so. When did Tokyo become the capital of Japan?
About 400 years ago.
—I see.... I got a good feel for the real Japan when I visited Kyoto and Osaka. Tokyo is indeed an international and modern city. But there is no 'Japan' in Tokyo.
Really?

▼Nakanoshima in Osaka

●Look & Learn

We Are Born Equal, But....

KAISHA

sha-chō

bu-chō

ka-chō

kakari-chō

(hira-)sha-in

DAIGAKU

gaku-chō

kyōju

jo-kyōju

kōshi

joshu

Japanese feel it is impolite to say the other person's name too much. So we often address the listener by his or her title. For example, students usually call their teacher "**sensei**," not "-san." So, "**Sha-chō wa soko e irasshaimasu ka?**" can mean either, 'Will our boss go there?' or 'Boss, will you go there?' Another way to avoid this impoliteness is to refer to people with place words. e. g. **kochira** ⟨this person⟩

New Words For UNIT 28

…ga,	…, but, although…, →KS
haikingu	〈Nv〉 ←hiking
kangae-kata	way of thinking
	kangae· think, consider
	-kata how to…
	→U-18 FS
…kara,	because…, →KS
	Cf. V·te kara after doing … →U-24
…keredomo,	though…, →KS
mada-mada	still more; far from being satisfactory
mata	again 〈also used as in

	parting as "See you again." →below〉
…na-n'desu	=na-nodesu →U-27 FS
naze	why? →KS
Rosu	←Los (Angeles)
Rosu-anjerusu	←Los Angeles
tazune·	to ask; visit
wariai	comparatively, quite, more or less
yasum·	to rest; have a holiday; be absent; go to bed
	Cf. yasumi rest

+·+·+·+·+·+·+·+·+·+·+·+·+·+·+·+·+

When Two Japanese Meet

Yā! 〈between men〉
Mā! 〈between women〉
Ara! 〈between women〉
Konnichiwa! 〈general〉
Kore wa, kore wa! 〈informal〉
Hāi! 〈between Americanized people〉
Hisashiburi! 〈after a long absence〉
Hajimemashite! 〈very formal; when meeting for the first time, usually followed by an exchange of name cards〉
Aitakatta! 〈between lovers〉
! 〈silence〉

When They Part

Jā! 〈friendly〉
Jā ne! 〈between young people〉
Jā, mata! 〈informal〉
Dewa, kore-de. 〈quite formal〉
Mata ne! 〈between young people〉
Bāi! 〈between Americanized people〉
Sayōnara! 〈general〉
Bai-bai! 〈between children〉
Sore-ja! 〈informal, but widely used〉
O-genki-de! 〈when they part for quite a long time〉
Sayoooonaraaaa! 〈when they part forever〉
! 〈silence〉

UNIT 28
To Indicate CAUSE And EFFECT

● **Key Structures**

1. Anata wa naze yasumimashita ka?
   —Byōki datta kara desu.
2. Byōki datta kara, yasumimashita.
3. Byōki datta keredomo, yasumimasen deshita.
4. Byōki deshita ga, gakkō e ikimashita.

---

1 | **... naze ... ka?** | why?

| [Sentence₁] **kara desu.** | Because [Sentence₁].

Aspect ⟨➡Unit 22 FS⟩ is expressed in the [Sentence].

2 | [Sentence₁] **kara,** [Sentence₂] | Because [S₁], [S₂]

3 | [Sentence₁] **keredomo,** [Sentence₂] | Although [S₁], [S₂]

There is one rule concerning the usage of Vᴾ/Plain Forms and Vᴹ/desu. Vᴹ/desu is to be used only once a sentence. Because this rule applies when you combine two sentences to make Compound Sentences as above, the Vᴾ/Plain Forms are preferred for ending [Sentence₁] and the Vᴹ/desu forms are saved for the end of the whole. ➡Unit 23 ②

4 | [Sentence₁] **ga,** [Sentence₂]

When ga is used to combine two sentences, the meaning is somewhat ambiguous. Although it usually means 'but,' it can also mean 'and' or 'so.'

1. Why were you absent?

   —Because I was ill.

2. I stayed home because I was sick.

3. Although I was ill, I did not stay home.

4. I was ill, but I went to school.

★More Examples For Practice

1. (Anata wa) **naze** Nippon e ikimashita **ka?**

   —Nippon-go o benkyō-shita·katta **kara** desu.

   Naze minna to haikingu ni ikimasen **ka?**

   —Tsukarete iru **kara** desu.

2. Watashi wa Nippon-go o benkyō-shitai **kara**, Nippon ni kimashita.

   Watashi wa tsukarete iru **kara**, minna to haikingu ni ikimasen.

   Michi ga wakaranakatta **kara**, keikan ni tazunemashita.

3. Tsukarete ita **keredomo**, haikingu ni ikimashita.

   Kinō wa yuki datta **keredomo**, sonna-ni samu·ku-na·katta desu.

4. Kinō wa yuki deshita **ga**, wariai atata-ka·katta desu.

   Tōkyō e ikimashita **ga**, Satō-san ni au-koto ga dekimasen deshita.

   Nippon-go wa muzukashi·i **ga**, omoshi-ro·i desu.

1. What did you go to Japan for?

   —Because I wanted to study Japanese.

   Why don't you go hiking with everybody else?

   —I'm tired.

2. I came to Japan so that I could study Japanese.

   Since I'm tired, I'm not going to go hiking with everybody else.

   Losing my way, I asked a policeman.

3. Although I was tired, I went hiking.

   It snowed yesterday, but it wasn't so cold.

4. It snowed yesterday, but it was rather warm.

   Though I went to Tokyo, I was unable to meet Mr. Sato.

   Japanese is difficult, but interesting.

● Further Study

Word Order

As you have seen, you have more freedom in Japanese word order than in English ⟨➡Unit 6 ①⟩. But, you have less freedom in the word order within a phrase. Here, the principal word order in a phrase will be reviewed and contrasted with English.

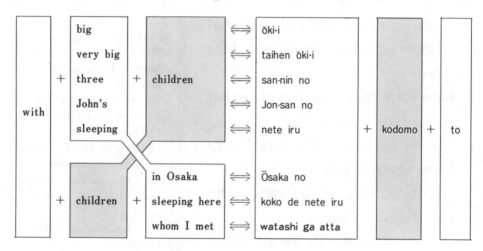

As the above chart shows, Japanese modifiers always precede the word they modify. ➡Unit 30 ①, ②, & FS

When an N is modified by two or more kinds of modifiers, you can put the modifiers in any order you like. But, the word order shown in Unit 2 FS is recommended as the most standard and therefore least confusing.

A Number functions just like an N, and you should put no after it to modify an N. In this case, you may have other possible word orders. You can choose the order 'N+Number+P⟨Postposition⟩' in place of 'Number no N+P' if the P is not ga, o, or wa. And if the P is ga or o, you can say 'N ga/o Number,' as in san-nin no kodomo to＝kodomo san-nin to or san-nin no kodomo ga/o＝kodomo ga/o san-nin.

●Conversation

MATA O-AI-SHITAI DESU NE. 《English and Japanese》

Sumisu-san, Nippon-go ga jōzu-ni
narimashita ne.

—Iie, mada-mada desu. Mō-sugu
 kuni ni kaeru-koto ni narimashita
 ga, kaette kara mo Nippon-go o
 benkyō-suru tsumori desu.
 Nippon-go wa Ei-go to taihen
 chigaimasu kara, muzukashi·i
 keredomo, omoshiro·i desu.
 Nippon-jin no kangae-kata ga yo·ku
 wakaru kara desu.

Watashi mo Ei-go ga jōzu-ni naritai
desu.

—Naze jōzu-ni naritai nodesu ka?

Rai-nen Amerika e iku-koto ni natte
iru kara desu.

—Sore wa shirimasen deshita.
 Amerika no dochira desu ka?

Rosu na-n'desu.

—E? Rosu-anjerusu desu ka?

Hai. Amerika de mata o-ai-shitai desu
ne.

Mr. Smith, you've become
very good at Japanese, really.
—No, not really. I have to
go back to the States soon,
but I think I'll study
Japanese some more there.
Japanese is completely
different from English, so
it's very difficult but in-
teresting.
It helps me understand the
Japanese way of thinking.
I wish I were as good at
English.
—Why do you want to be
good at English?
I'm supposed to go to the
States next year.
—I didn't know that.
Which part of the States?
'Rosu.'
—Pardon? Oh, Los Angeles?
Yes. I hope we meet again
in the States.

●Look & Learn

Japanese Orthography

To tell the truth, Japanese is not usually written in ABC. So far, you have been learning Japanese written in such an alphabet, and we believe this form is perfectly adequate for preparing you to take part on either side of a normal conversation, but it will do nothing for you when it comes time for reading or writing real Japanese.

We are sorry not to have introduced the written language before this, but, as a glance at any magazine or newspaper will make obvious, the omission had its reasons. Now, however, it is time to get your feet wet. You do not need to memorize the basic script on pages 190–191, but please look it over and try to get used to the shapes of written Japanese.

(1) To begin with, Japanese did not have any writing system until Chinese Ideograms were adopted about fifteen centuries ago. We still use some Chinese Ideograms ⟨KANJI⟩.

Ancient Chinese sound: kǎ

Chinese meaning: to add

(2) After a while Japanese began to simplify the original Chinese Ideograms and to use them to indicate the sounds of Japanese as well. This simplification, or Japanization, of Chinese Ideograms took two forms, KATAKANA and HIRAGANA.

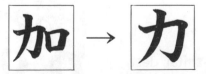 &

Japanese
sound: ka

KATAKANA is used today for emphasis or foreign words, like italics in English. HIRAGANA is used most widely.

New Words For UNIT 29

aida	① X to Y no aida 〈N〉 between X and Y 〈Time/Space〉 ② ...no aida 〈N〉 among...; during... ③ ... aida while... →KS
...ato	after... →KS
-chū	〈N/Adv〉 all through [Time] →FS
...go	〈N/Adv〉 ...later →FS
hoshi	star, planet
-jū	〈N/Adv〉 all through [Time/Space] →FS
jūsho	address
-ka-getsu	〈N/Adv〉 ...months →FS
-ka-getsu-kan	〈N/Adv〉 for...months Cf. Ni-gatsu February; ni-ka-getsu two months; ni-ka-getsu-kan for two months →FS
-kan	for [Time]; between/among [Space] e.g. Watashi wa san-nen-kan Nippon ni imashita. I was in Japan for three years.; Shinkansen wa Tōkyō-Hakata-kan o hashitte imasu. The Shinkansen runs between Tokyo and Hakata.
mae	① X no mae ni before X 〈Time/Place/Action〉 ② ... mae [Period of time] ago/ before 〈N/Adv〉 e.g. yon-ka-getsu mae four months ago →FS
-nen-kan	〈N/Adv〉 for...years →FS
o-sewa	〈Nv〉 care (=sewa) o-sewa ni nar· 〈Cph〉 to receive others' kindness/ care e.g. O-sewa ni nari-masu. Thank you for your kindness/care. 〈when you are to benefit from, or are

benefitting from, the other person's kindness〉
O-sewa ni narimashita. Thank you for your kind-ness/care. 〈when you have benefitted from the other person's kindness〉
Cf. **Arigatō** gozaimasu. vs. **Arigatō** gozaimashita.
...no (o-)sewa o suru take care of...

rusu	〈Nv〉 staying away from home, being not at home
sabishi·i	lonely, lonesome
-sai	〈Counter Suffix for a per-son's or an animal's age〉 〈N〉 e.g. is-sai one year old; has-sai/hachi-sai eight years old; jus-sai ten years old; hatachi twenty years old; ni-jū-is-sai twenty-one years old
sewa	〈Nv〉 care →o-sewa
shōchi	〈Nv〉 agreement, consent
sotsugyō	〈Nv〉 graduation
tat·	to start, leave (on a trip) (=shuppatsu-suru) Cf. tat· to stand up
toki	〈N〉 time
yoroshi·i	OK, right, suitable yoroshi·ku 〈Cph〉 as you think fit 〈when you are introduced to someone, or when you send your re-gards to someone〉 Dōzo yoroshi·ku. 〈Cph〉 Please (continue your fa-vors toward me) appropri-ately. ...ni yoroshi·ku (Please give my best regards) to ... appropriately.

UNIT 29
To Say WHEN

● Key Structures

1. Kodomo no toki, Burajiru e itta koto ga arimasu.
2. Shizuka-na toki ni, benkyō-shimasu.
3. Anata ga koko e kita toki, watashi wa hon o yonde imashita.
4. Nippon ni iru aida ni, Nippon-go o benkyō-shimashita.
5. Nippon e kuru mae ni, Nippon-go o benkyō-shimashita.
6. Yoshida-san ga kaetta ato, Tanaka-san ga kimashita.

---

1 | N no/Na/A·i toki (ni) | when N/Na/A

2 | Vᴾ toki (ni) | when someone does/did...

When V·ta or V·nakatta is used as Vᴾ, it means 'has/had (not) done...' and does not necessarily means the past tense. ➜ Unit 22 FS

e.g. Nippon e iku toki, Jon-san ni aimashita.

    ⟨When I was going to Japan, I met John.⟩

    Nippon e itta toki, Tanaka-san ni aimasu.

    ⟨When I get to Japan, I'll meet Mr. Tanaka.⟩

3 | N no/Na/A·i/Vᴾ aida (ni) | while N/Na/A/V

4 | N no/V·u mae ni | before N/V

5 | N no/V·ta ato (de) | after N/V

1. I once went to Brazil when I was little.

2. I study when it is quiet.

3. When you came here, I was reading a book.

4. While I was in Japan, I studied Japanese.

5. Before I came to Japan, I had studied Japanese.

6. After Yoshida left, Tanaka came.

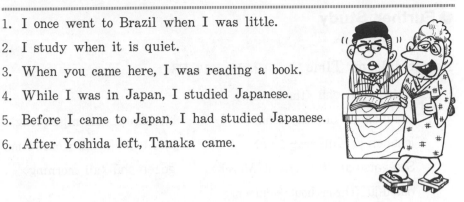

★More Examples For Practice

1. Ni-jū-roku-sai **no toki** kekkon-shima-shita.

   Byōki **no toki ni**wa, sugu byōin e itta hō ga i·i desu.

   Atsu·**i toki**, bīru ga oishi·i desu.

   Sabishi·**i toki**, tomodachi ga hoshi·i.

   Yoru sora no kirei-**na toki**, hoshi ga yo·ku miemasu.

2. Amerika kara Nippon ni **kuru toki**, Hawai ga miemashita.

   Amerika kara Nippon ni **kita toki**, Fuji-san ga miemashita.

3. Anata no rusu **no aida ni**, Ōta-san ga kimashita.

4. Ryokō **no mae ni**, kaimono o shitai desu.

5. Eiga **no ato de**, shokuji-shimashita.

   Sotsugyō-**shita ato**, nani o shitai?

---

1. I got married when I was 26.
   When you get sick, you should go to the hospital as soon as possible.
   Beer is good when it is hot.
   When I'm lonely, I want a friend.
   When the sky is clear at night, you can see the stars clearly.

2. On my way from the States to Japan, I saw Hawaii.
   When I got to Japan from the States, I saw Mt. Fuji.

3. Ota came while you were out.

4. I want to go shopping before I go on my trip.

5. After the movies we had something to eat.
   What do you want to do after graduation?

● Further Study

Adverbials of Time   Cf. Unit 17 FS

I. Duration: -jū/-chū ⟨throughout⟩

    ichi-nichi-jū ⟨all day long⟩   hitoban-jū ⟨all night long⟩

    ichi-nen-jū ⟨all year long⟩   hito-tsuki-jū ⟨all month long⟩

    San-gatsu-jū ⟨throughout March⟩   gozen-chū ⟨all morning⟩

    natsu-jū ⟨throughout summer⟩

    kotoshi-jū ⟨all this year⟩

    kon-shū-jū ⟨all this week⟩

II. Duration: -kan ⟨for⟩

    [Number]-ka-getsu-kan ⟨for one month, two months, etc.⟩

      NB: 'One month,' 'ten months,' and 'eleven months' are ik-ka-getsu, juk-ka-getsu, and jū-ik-ka-getsu respectively.

    [Day of a Month]-kan ⟨for one day, two days, etc.⟩

      NB: 'For one day' is ichi-nichi, not ichi-nichi-kan or tsuitachi-kan.

    [Number]-nen-kan ⟨for one year, two years, etc.⟩

      NB: 'For four years' is yo-nen-kan.

    [Number]-shū-kan ⟨for one week, two weeks, etc.⟩

      NB: 'One week,' 'eight weeks,' and 'ten weeks' are is-shū-kan, has-shū-kan, and jus-shū-kan respectively.

III. 'Sometime during...': -jū/-chū ni ➡ I.

    e.g. kotoshi-jū ni ⟨sometime this year⟩

IV. 'Ago' and 'Later': mae (ni) and go/nochi (ni)

    e.g. mik-ka mae ⟨three days ago⟩

         ik-ka-getsu mae ⟨one month ago⟩

         san-shū-kan go ⟨three weeks later⟩

         jū-nen nochi ⟨ten years later⟩

●Conversation

O-SEWA NI NARIMASHITA.———《Good-by, Friend!》

—Nippon ni iru aida, taihen o-sewa
ni narimashita.

Iie, dō-itashimashite.

—Anata ga rai-nen Amerika ni kuru
toki, zehi renraku-shite kudasai.
Kore wa watashi no Amerika no
jūsho desu.

Arigatō. Itsu tachimasu ka?

—Asu no asa hachi-ji ni tachimasu.
Nippon o tatsu mae ni, Satō-san
ni aitai nodesu ga, au-koto ga
dekimasen. Satō-san ni yoroshi·ku.

Hai, wakarimashita.

—Sore-kara, imōto no Kyashī wa
ima, Hokkaidō no ato, Shikoku o
ryokō-shite imasu. Tōkyō e kaette
kita toki, sumimasen ga kono
tegami o watashite kudasai.

Hai, shōchi-shimashita.

Sore-ja, dōzo o-genki-de.

—Thank you for everything
while I've been here.
Don't mention it.
—When you come to the
States next year, be sure
to get in touch with me.
This is my address in the
States.
Thanks. When do you leave?
—I'm leaving at eight tomor-
row morning.
I want to meet Mr. Sato
before I leave Japan, but
it doesn't look like I'll be
able to.
Please give him my best.
Certainly.
—And, my sister Cathy is
traveling in Shikoku after
her trip to Hokkaido.
When she gets back to
Tokyo, would you please
give this letter to her?
Yes, sure.
Well, then, have a good trip!

▼Mashu-ko in Hokkaido

●Look & Learn

This Is What Real Japanese Looks Like.

第1部 歴史のかたち

て働いたにちがいない。いやおそらく、この信仰と強制の両者が同時に働いていたのである。おもしろいことに、歴史のあけぼのに立ったシュメールでもエジプトでも、開拓された土地は神の領地であった。[5] そしてこの神の名代をつとめたのは、少数者の支配する精鋭な経済的・政治的制度であった。

アフラシアの河川流域を開拓して農地としたのは、精神的生気としては信仰であり、指導力としては政治的権威、技術的装備であり、これらをともにそなえたこの訓練された共同作業だった。「紀元前5000年ないし4000年において今とはいちじるしく異なる降雨量や天候のパターンがあったとは思えない以上、メソポタミアの沖積地における広範囲にわたる生活は、灌漑というものを抜きにしては文字どおり不可能であっただろう」[*ブレッドウッド、前掲書][6]。「大河流域の沖積地はほかのところよりも苛酷な環境であったが、しかし同時にこれを開発すればより大きな物的報酬を約束する土地でもあった。この土地において銅器時代の村落は青銅器時代の都市に変貌したのである」[*前田、チャイルド『歴史に何が起こったか』]。「食糧生産の革命はおそらく人類史の転回点であった。しか…の諸結果が実現されたのは、都市革命を通じてで…文明の初期の業績のうちもっとも…もの──すなわち、ティグリ…地を変じてシュメールの国土…たもっとも早い時期の東…

一つの応答であったことがわかる。小オアシスをいくつか開墾することは、この挑戦にたいする最初の応答であったわけだが、しかし、やがてそれだけでは、アフラシアは後雨期の気候条件下で人間が永住できる土地とはなりえないことがわかってきた。けっきょく人間は次の二者択一を迫られることになった。一つは移住であり、この道をえらんだ先駆者たちは農業をアフラシアから旧世界の端まで伝えた。他の一つはアフラシアの沼地の開拓であり、これをついになし遂げた者が、もっとも初期の旧世界文明の創造者となった。沼地の開拓というのは永続的な解決策であった。というのは、こうして耕作可能となった新しい土地は河川によって永久的に灌漑されるからだ。その河川は乾燥地帯からはずれたところに源を発し、したがって、水の浸蝕作用による沈泥が事実無尽蔵に供給されるわけで、大地は、こうして永久にうるおったのである。開拓された流域地帯では、規律をもって組織的に重労働をつづけるかぎり、人間は暮しの目途をたてることができた。

乾燥というのが挑戦であった。シュメールとエジプトの国…がそれにたいする応答だった。だが、ただこう述べただけ…いるわけで誤解をうむだろう。

New Words For UNIT 30

...de-aru — who is/are... →FS

kata — person 〈cannot be used independently, but is always modified. Honorific expression.
e.g. kono kata=kochira 〈→U-27 LL〉=kono hito 〈Impolite〉〉

kūkō — airport
Cf. hikō-jō (local) airport; Although most facilities in international airports in Japan are indicated in English, it may be useful to know some Japanese expressions, such as: Kokusai-sen International Routes; Kokunai-sen Domestic Routes; Zeikan Customs; Ryōgae Money Exchange; Hoteru-annai-jo Hotel Information Machiai-shitsu Waiting Room Menzei-ten Duty-Free Shop

kyaku — customer, guest

mai-ban — every night

natsukashi·i — not easily forgettable, dear, fondly remembered

o-kyaku-san — =kyaku

onaji — the same 〈Though this is N, it can be used as Adj. Neg. →onaji dewa na·i= chigaw·〉
e.g. Watashi no nekutai to anata no wa onaji desu. My necktie is the same (type/color, etc.) as yours. Kore to onaji nekutai o misete kudasai. Show me a necktie like this one. Watashi to anata wa onaji toshi ni umaremashita. You and I were born in the same year.

Oya? — Oh!; Gee!

shimar· — to close 〈Vi〉
Cf. shime· to close 〈Vt〉

taipisuto — ←typist

tōr· — pass; go through

▼New Tokyo International Airport(Narita)

UNIT 30
To MODIFY Nouns

● Key Structures

1. nete iru kodomo

2. soko de nete iru kodomo

3. watashi ga kinō atta hito

4. oji-san ga watashi ni kureta hon

5. me ga ugoku ningyō

---

1 $\boxed{\text{V}^\text{P} \text{ N}}$

V$^\text{P}$ can modify N.

2 $\boxed{\text{[Sentence] N}}$

Most of the Constructions, except those in Unit 23, Unit 28, and Unit 29, have been Simple Sentences. So perhaps you would like to know how to modify N with sentences. In English you have very complicated rules about 'relatives' such as which, of which, whose, whomever, where, whereof, how, etc. Forget them! Japanese is very, very simple. As you can see in 1, V$^\text{P}$ can modify N, and Japanese Verbs/desu come at the end of the sentence. You simply change V$^\text{M}$/desu into V$^\text{P}$/Plain Forms and put [Sentence] just before N. That's all. There are, however, some other rules to observe in this Construction. →FS

*　　　*　　　*

Finally, we do not want to discourage you, but, please be careful: It is the games with the simplest rules that are the hardest to master. Please think of this text as merely a rule book, a simple introduction to the difficult game of mastering Japanese.

1. a sleeping child
2. a child sleeping there
3. the person I met yesterday
4. the book my uncle gave me
5. the doll with movable eyes

★More Examples For Practice

1. tonde iku hikō-ki

   tonde iru hikō-ki

   orite kuru hikō-ki

   aite iru mado

   shimatte iru doa

2. jū-nen mae ni shinda chichi

   jū-nen-kan hataraite iru hito

   jū-nen-kan hataraite iru kaisha

   asu no gogo au hito

   kyō no gogo Ōta-san ni au hito

   anata ga mita eiga

   watashi ga yonda hon

   anata ga hon o ageta hito

   anata ni hon o kureta hito

   anata ga Hawai e issho-ni iku hito

   Satō-san no hoshi·i jidōsha

   jidōsha ga hoshi·i Satō-san

   kami ga naga·i wakamono-tachi

   gorufu ga jōzu-na Suzuki-san

   taipisuto de-aru/no Ōta-san

1. plane taking off
   flying plane
   plane coming in for a landing
   open window
   closed door
2. father who died ten years ago
   man who has been working for 10 years
   company where I've been working for 10 years
   man whom I'll meet tomorrow afternoon
   man who'll meet Ota this afternoon
   movie which you saw
   book which I read
   man whom you gave a book to
   man who gave you a book
   man you go to Hawaii with
   car which Sato wants
   Sato who wants a car
   young people with long hair
   Suzuki who is good at golf
   Ota, a typist

● Further Study

Summary of Pre-Noun Modifiers

I. Words and Phrases Modifying N

    (1) kono/sono/ano/dono   ➡U-2 ③, U-3 FS, & U-15 FS

    (2) konna/sonna/anna/donna   ➡U-15 FS

    (3) N no/Na/A·i   ➡U-2 ① & ②

    (4) V^P ➡U-14 FS

    (5) Plain Forms of N/N(a)/A·i desu   ➡U-23 FS

    NB: De-aru is used instead of da.

II. N₁ wa N₂ ga... Constructions ⟨➡U-26 FS⟩ Modifying N

    (1) N₁ no... N₂

        The part '...' should be transformed as in I.

        e.g. Watashi wa inu ga suki desu. ⟨I like dogs.⟩

              →watashi no suki de-aru inu ⟨dogs which I like⟩

                watashi no suki-na inu ⟨dogs which I like⟩

    (2) N₂ ga... N₁

        The part '...' should be transformed as in I.

        e.g. Keiko-san wa neko ga suki desu. ⟨Keiko likes cats.⟩

              →neko ga suki de-aru Keiko-san ⟨Keiko who likes cats⟩

                neko ga suki-na Keiko-san ⟨Keiko who likes cats⟩

III. Other Sentences

    Sentence endings should be transformed as in I. and wa should
    be replaced by ga or o. ➡U-19 ③ & FS

        e.g. Tanaka-san wa isha desu. ⟨Mr. Tanaka is a doctor.⟩

              →isha de-aru Tanaka-san ⟨Mr. Tanaka who is a doctor⟩

                isha no Tanaka-san ⟨Mr. Tanaka who is a doctor⟩

●Conversation

NATSUKASHI·I HON DESU.————《Leaving Japan》

—Kūkō made.

Kōsoku-dōro o tōtte mo yoroshi·i desu ka?

—I·i desu yo. Oya? Kono takushī wa watashi ga Nippon e kita toki notta onaji takushī desu ne.

E? Ā, omoidashimashita. Ano toki no o-kyaku-san desu ne.

Amerika no kata desu ka?

—Sō desu.

Shikashi, Nippon-go ga o-jōzu desu ne.

—Iya, kita toki wa, zenzen wakari-masen deshita. Kono hon de benkyō-shita n'desu yo.

Doko no hon desu ka?

—Gakken no tekisuto desu.

　Mai-ban yonde benkyō-shita hon desu. Natsukashi·i hon desu.

O-kyaku-san, kūkō desu.

* * *

—SAYŌNARA, NIPPON!

—To the airport, please.

Can we take the toll road?

—Yes. Hey! This is the same cab I took when I came to Japan!

What? Oh, I remember. You're that person!

Are you American?

—Yes, I am.

But you speak Japanese very well.

—No, I didn't understand Japanese at all when I came. I used this book to study with.

Who published the book?

—This is a textbook published by Gakken. This is the book I read and studied every evening. My dear book....

Here we are at the airport.

* * *

—Good-by, Japan!

▼A taxicab

APPENDIX I

Japanese Syllabary Chart

HIRAGANA

あ a	か ka	が ga	さ sa	ざ za	た ta	だ da	な na	は ha	ば ba	ぱ pa	ま ma	ら ra	わ wa	ん n
い i	き ki	ぎ gi	し shi	じ ji	ち chi	ぢ ji	に ni	ひ hi	び bi	ぴ pi	み mi	り ri		
う u	く ku	ぐ gu	す su	ず zu	つ tsu	づ zu	ぬ nu	ふ fu	ぶ bu	ぷ pu	む mu	る ru		
え e	け ke	げ ge	せ se	ぜ ze	て te	で de	ね ne	へ he	べ be	ぺ pe	め me	れ re		
お o	こ ko	ご go	そ so	ぞ zo	と to	ど do	の no	ほ ho	ぼ bo	ぽ po	も mo	ろ ro		を o
や ya	きゃ kya	ぎゃ gya	しゃ sha	じゃ ja	ちゃ cha	ぢゃ ja	にゃ nya	ひゃ hya	びゃ bya	ぴゃ pya	みゃ mya	りゃ rya		
ゆ yu	きゅ kyu	ぎゅ gyu	しゅ shu	じゅ ju	ちゅ chu	ぢゅ ju	にゅ nyu	ひゅ hyu	びゅ byu	ぴゅ pyu	みゅ myu	りゅ ryu		
よ yo	きょ kyo	ぎょ gyo	しょ sho	じょ jo	ちょ cho	ぢょ jo	にょ nyo	ひょ hyo	びょ byo	ぴょ pyo	みょ myo	りょ ryo		

NB: 1) These charts show almost all the beats (→p.7) of current Japanese and how to express them in HIRAGANA and KATAKANA.

2) Long vowels in HIRAGANA are expressed by adding the vowel letter あ, う, え, or お.
e.g. おかあさん okā-san, ゆうがた yūgata, おねえさん onē-san, おおきい ōki·i
The extended ō is in some cases expressed by adding う instead of お.
e.g. おとうさん otō-san

3) Long vowels in KATAKANA are expressed by ー.
e.g. デパート depāto, キー kī, ウール ūru〈wool〉, テーブル tēburu, コーヒー kōhī

4) When a syllable ends in a consonant, a small っ(ッ) is used to express the consonant if it is not n.
e.g. いった itta, がっこう gakkō, いっち itchi〈accord〉
マッチ matchi, ストッキング sutokkingu

5) The Postpositions e, o, and wa are, respectively, expressed by へ(へ),

KATAKANA

ア a	カ ka	ガ ga	サ sa	ザ za	タ ta	ダ da	ナ na	ハ ha	バ ba	パ pa	マ ma	ラ ra	ワ wa	ファ fa	ン n
イ i	キ ki	ギ gi	シ shi	ジ ji	チ chi	ヂ ji	ニ ni	ヒ hi	ビ bi	ピ pi	ミ mi	リ ri		フィ fi	
ウ u	ク ku	グ gu	ス su	ズ zu	ツ tsu	ヅ zu	ヌ nu	フ fu	ブ bu	プ pu	ム mu	ル ru			
エ e	ケ ke	ゲ ge	セ se	ゼ ze	テ te	デ de	ネ ne	ヘ he	ベ be	ペ pe	メ me	レ re		フェ fe	
オ o	コ ko	ゴ go	ソ so	ゾ zo	ト to	ド do	ノ no	ホ ho	ボ bo	ポ po	モ mo	ロ ro		フォ fo	ヲ o
ヤ ya	キャ kya	ギャ gya	シャ sha	ジャ ja	チャ cha	ヂャ ja	ニャ nya	ヒャ hya	ビャ bya	ピャ pya	ミャ mya	リャ rya			
ユ yu	キュ kyu	ギュ gyu	シュ shu	ジュ ju	チュ chu	ヂュ ju	ニュ nyu	ヒュ hyu	ビュ byu	ピュ pyu	ミュ myu	リュ ryu			
ヨ yo	キョ kyo	ギョ gyo	ショ sho	ジョ jo	チョ cho	ヂョ jo	ニョ nyo	ヒョ hyo	ビョ byo	ピョ pyo	ミョ myo	リョ ryo			

を (ヲ), and は(ハ) instead of え (エ), お (オ), and わ (ワ)

e.g. かいしゃへ kaisha e, てがみを tegami o, わたしは watashi wa

6) The letter じ(ジ), not ぢ(ヂ), is always used to express the sound ji except where the sound chi is changed into ji in a compound word or the sound ji is preceded by the sound chi in one word. In such cases, ぢ (ヂ) is used.

e.g. はなぢ hanaji〈nosebleed〉〔←hana + chi〈blood〉〕, ちぢみ chijimi〈crêpe〉

By the same token, the letter ず is preferred to づ.

7) The sound f followed by all vowels but u in a loan word in KATAKANA can be expressed as shown in the above chart.

e.g. オフィス ofisu

8) The sound ti in a loan word in KATAKANA is expressed by the letter テ with a small イ following.

e.g. ビューティフルな byūtifuru-na

APPENDIX II

Let's Read Japanese

●Part 1 HIRAGANA

あい 〈Nv〉 love   いえ house   いいえ No,   うえ 〈N〉 upper part
あおい blue   あう to meet   いう to say   おおい many

♦ NB: Long vowels are expressed by adding the vowel letter あ，う，え，or お.
　　→APPENDIX I NB: 2)
　　e.g. おおい is pronounced more like ōi than o-oi.

か ka き ki く ku け ke こ ko

ここ 〈N〉 here   えき station   くうき air 〈kūki, not ku-uki〉
かく to write   きく to hear   あき autumn   あかい red
いけ pond   けいこ 〈Nv〉 practice 〈kēko, rather than ke-iko〉

すし *sushi*   そこ 〈N〉 there   あそこ 〈N〉 over there
あさ morning   けさ this morning   あす tomorrow
せかい world   おそい late; slow   けしき scenery

た ta ち chi つ tsu て te と to

ちち my father   つき moon   そと 〈N〉 outside
くつした socks   ちかてつ subway   たかい high; expensive
とけい clock, watch   とおい far 〈tōi, not to-oi〉

♦ NB: A double consonant (other than n) is expressed by a small っ.
　　→APPENDIX I NB: 4)
　　e.g. あさって the day after tomorrow 〈asatte〉
　　　　きっと without fail; surely 〈kitto〉
　　　　かった bought 〈katta〉←かう

な na	に ni	ぬ nu	ね ne	の no

なに what(?)　　ねこ cat　　こねこ kitten　　いぬ dog
こいぬ puppy　　かに crab　　おかね money　　にく meat
ぬの cloth　　ななつ seven　　ここのつ nine　　この, その, あの

は ha	ひ hi	ふ fu	へ he	ほ ho

はは my mother　　ふね ship　　ひこうき airplane
はね feather　　はなし story　　はなす to speak; to let go
ほそい slender　　あさひ morning sun　　へた 〈Na〉 unskillful
♦NB: The Postposition wa is expressed by は, not わ.
　　　e.g. このひとは…　　ここは…　　あなたのいえは…
　　　The Postposition e is expressed by へ, not え.
　　　e.g. はこねへいく to go to Hakone

ま ma	み mi	む mu	め me	も mo

なまえ name　　うみ ocean　　むすめ daughter; girl
すむ to live　　おもう to think　　つめたい cold
さむい cold　　もしもし Hello,　　おもい heavy
のむ to drink　　まえ 〈N/Adv〉 front; before

ら ra	り ri	る ru	れ re	ろ ro

はる spring　　あたらしい new　　きれい 〈Na〉 clean; pretty
かれら they　　ひる midday; daytime　　れきし history
ひろい wide　　おてら Buddhist temple　　くろい black
くらい dark　　きらい 〈Na〉 detestable　　おりる to get off, descend
これ, それ, あれ　　これら, それら, あれら

を o

おかねをはらう to pay the money　　なまえをかく to write the name
♦NB: This letter is used exclusively for the Postposition o.

わ wa

わかい young	わたし I	わるい bad
かわ river	わすれる to forget	すわる to sit down
にわ garden	わかれる to part	へいわ peace

♦ NB: There are no letters shown for the sounds wi, wu, we, and wo since these pronunciations are not used in modern Japanese.

ん n

ほん book	けいかん policeman	かんたん ⟨Na⟩ simple
きけん ⟨Na⟩ dangerous	なんかい how often(?)	けんか ⟨Nv⟩ quarrel
れんらく ⟨Nv⟩ contact	かんけい ⟨Nv⟩ relation	きんえん No Smoking
せんせい teacher	しんせつ ⟨Na⟩ kind	おんせん spa, hot spring
こんな, そんな, あんな		

や ya   ゆ yu   よ yo

ふゆ winter	ゆき snow	よる night
よい good	ゆうめい ⟨Na⟩ famous	ほんやさん bookshop
にちよう Sunday	おはよう Good morning.	やすい inexpensive
よてい ⟨Nv⟩ plan	はやい speedy, early	よこ ⟨N⟩ side
やくそく ⟨Nv⟩ promise	ゆうかん evening paper	りよう ⟨Nv⟩ utilize

♦ NB: There are no letters shown for the sounds yi and ye since these pronunciations are not used in modern Japanese.

❶ The small や may be attached to certain letters to make the following sounds.

きゃ kya	しゃ sha	ちゃ cha	にゃ nya
ひゃ hya	みゃ mya	りゃ rya	

かいしゃ company   きしゃ locomotive, train
こうちゃ black tea   ひゃっかてん department store

❷ The small ゆ may be attached to certain letters to make the following sounds.

きゅ kyu	しゅ shu	ちゅ chu	にゅ nyu
ひゅ hyu	みゅ myu	りゅ ryu	

しゅと capital city   にゅういん 〈Nv〉 being hospitalized
ちゅうい 〈Nv〉 caution   りゅうこう 〈Nv〉 fashion, vogue
しゅうかん custom; week   きゅうこう express train

❸ The small ょ may be attached to certain letters to make the following sounds.

きょ kyo	しょ sho	ちょ cho	にょ nyo
ひょ hyo	みょ myo	りょ ryo	

きょう today   とうきょう Tokyo   りょうり 〈Nv〉 cooking
りょかん inn   しょうせつ novel   いきましょう Let's go.

が ga	ぎ gi	ぐ gu	げ ge	ご go		ぎゃ gya	ぎゅ gyu	ぎょ gyo
ざ za	じ ji	ず zu	ぜ ze	ぞ zo		じゃ ja	じゅ ju	じょ jo
ば ba	び bi	ぶ bu	べ be	ぼ bo		びゃ bya	びゅ byu	びょ byo
ぱ pa	ぴ pi	ぷ pu	ぺ pe	ぽ po		ぴゃ pya	ぴゅ pyu	ぴょ pyo
だ da	(ぢ ji)	(づ zu)	で de	ど do				

➡APPENDIX I NB: 6)

ぎんこう bank   がっこう school   えいご English
めがね glasses   にっぽん Japan   だいじょうぶ all right
だんだん gradually   ときどき sometimes   ごご afternoon
かばん bag   たべる to eat   どうぞ please
べんり 〈Na〉 useful   びんぼう 〈Na〉 poverty がか painter, artist
びょうき 〈N〉 illness, disease   おばあさん grandmother, old lady

●Part 2 KATAKANA

Study APPENDIX I (page 191) carefully. KATAKANA is used mainly for loan words (except Chinese, in which case KANJI is used). That's why you'll see some KATAKANA combinations like ファ, フィ, フェ, フォ, or ティ on page 191 even though you cannot find their HIRAGANA equivalents on page 190.

*   *   *

カメラ camera	ステレオ stereo set	パイプ pipe
オフィス office	マッチ match	コーヒー coffee
ペン pen	ライター lighter	テレビ television
ラジオ radio	ニュース news	パンダ panda
パーティー party	ゴルフ golf	ジャズ jazz
ノート notebook	レコード record	ステーキ steak
ビジネス business	ファッション fashion	ケーキ cake
スタジオ studio	ジーンズ jeans	タイピスト typist
アメリカ America	ブラジル Brazil	イギリス England
オーストラリア Australia	ニュージーランド New Zealand	
デパート department store	ルームサービス room service	
スーツケース suitcase	スポーツカー sports car	
テープレコーダー tape recorder	ジャンボジェット jumbo jet	

●Part 3 ...and KANJI?

Open the supplement that comes with this textbook. You can already read approximately 80% of what's there now that you've learned HIRAGANA and KATAKANA. But what about that other 20% that's in KANJI?

That's easy too. As a start, you can easily find the pronunciations in the main text with no trouble, and after a while you'll get so adept at recognizing these common KANJI that you won't even need to look them up. Soon you'll be able to read them for both sound and meaning without even breaking stride. Not only will you be ready to start learning KANJI, you'll have a head start. Remember: It's only hard if you think it's hard.

APPENDIX III

INDEX

♦This Index gives the pages on which each word appears prominently, with the more important page numbers in bold-face type.

ichi	44
ichiban	95
ichi-do	113
ichi-do-mo	107
Ichi-gatsu	50
ichiji	89
ichi-ji	41
ichi-man	44
ichi-nichi	110, 182
ie	17
Igirisu	11
Igirisu-jin	16
i·i	29
Iie,	11, 48, 50
ijime·	77
ik·	53, 155
ikaga	149
ike	131
ike·	83
Ikeda	149
ik-ka-getsu	110, 182
ik-kai ⟨floor⟩	41
ik-kai ⟨time⟩	110
ikura	17, 32
ikutsu	32
ima	41
imōto	52, 53
imōto-san	52
-in	23
inaka ⟨→tokai⟩	95
inochi	113
inor·	113
intāchenji	131
intānashonaru-na	149
inu	11
Irasshaimase.	23
irasshaimasu	41
ire·	59
iriguchi	77
iroiro-na	149
isha	23
isog·	53
isogashi·i	89
issho-ni	59
is-shū-kan	110, 182
isu	11
ita·i	161
Itaria	143
Itō	95
itsu	32, 41
itsu-demo	110, 143

Itsuka	50
itsu-made-mo	131
itsu-mo	59
itsutsu	44
iw·	143
Iya,	89

J

Jā,	53
Jā, mata.	59
janbo-jetto	71
Jā ne!	173
Jē-tī-bī	35
jetto-ki	125
-ji	41, 44
jibiinkō-ka	161
jibun-de	113
jidōsha	17
jikan	149
jin	95
-jin	11
jinja	47
jinkō	161
jī-pan	71
jitensha	35
Jitsu-wa,	149
jiyū	71
-jō	41
jo-kyōju	167
Jon	17
Jōnzu	11
josei	161
joshu	167
jōzu-na	113
jū	44
-jū	161, 179, 182
jūbun	131
Jū-gatsu	50
jū-go	44
jū-hachi	44
jū-ichi	44
Jū-ichi-gatsu	50
jū-ichi-ji	44
Jū-ichi-nichi	50
jū-ichi-nin	44
jū-ik-kai	44
jū-ji	41
juk-kai	44
jū-ku	44
Jū-ku-nichi	50

jū-kyū	44
jū-nana	44
jū-ni	44
Jū-ni-gatsu	50
jū-ni-ji	41
jū-ni-kai	44
jū-nin	44
jū-ni-nin	44
junsa	23
jū-roku	44
jū-san	44
jū-san-gai	44
jū-san-nin	44
jū-shi	44
jū-shichi	44
jūsho	179
jus-sai ⟨→-sai⟩	179
jūsu	125
Jū-yokka	50
jū-yon	44
jū-yo-nin	44
jū-yon-kai	44

K

ka	11
. . .ka?	29
-ka ⟨-or, -er, -ist⟩	23
-ka ⟨some~⟩	32
kaban	41
kabin	35
Kabuki	107
ka-chō	167
kado	155
kādo	113
kaer·	53
kaeri	116
-ka-getsu	107, 179
-ka-getsu-kan	179
. . .kai?	170
-kai ⟨floor⟩	41, 44
-kai ⟨times⟩	107, 110
kaigan	131
-kai-me	119
kaimono	149
kaisha	17
kaisha-in	23
kaiwa	143
kak·	53
kakari-chō	167
Kamakura	101, 112

APPENDIX IV

Index Of Grammatical Signs

♦The bold-face numbers indicate the pages showing how to make them.